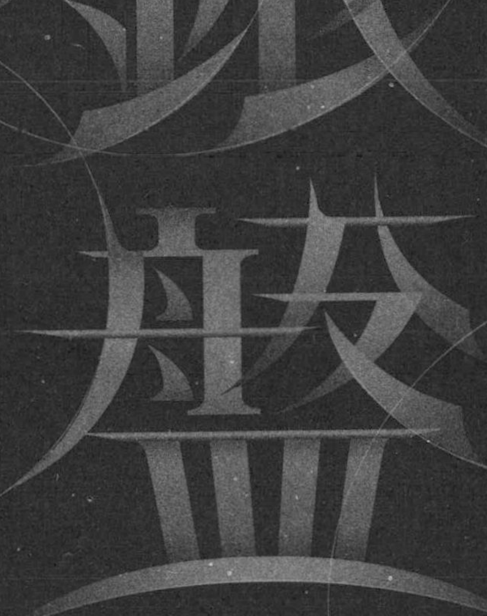

銀盤騎士

2

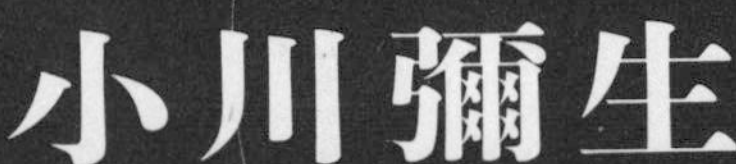

小川彌生

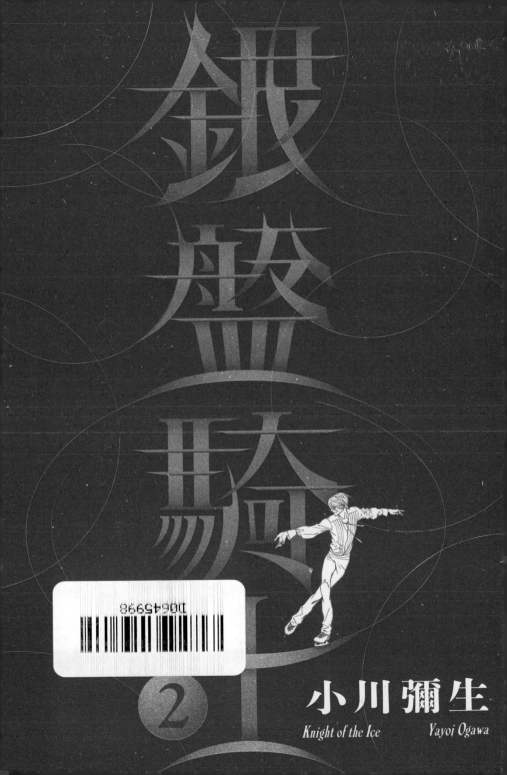

Knight of the Ice

Yayoi Ogawa

Characters

Kokoro Kijinami

The number one candidate to be Japan's next top men's figure skater. One of his greatest strengths is the beauty his height lends to his quadruple jumps. He cracks easily under pressure, but he's gotten more consistent since Chitose started reciting a magic spell for him.

Chitose Igari

An editor for the health-and-lifestyle magazine *SASSO*. She's so short that she often gets mistaken for an elementary schooler, but she's actually 23 and has been out of college for two years. She's also Kokoro's childhood friend and calls him Kokoppe, while he calls her Se-chan.

Magical Princess Lady Lala is a magical girl anime that was on TV eleven years ago. Chitose and Kokoro loved it, and they often played pretend as the characters.

Yayoi Ogata

A manga artist. She went to the same college as Chitose and knows about her relationship to Kokoro.

Sawada

The head of the editorial department for Kodan Publishing's magazine *SASSO*. He's good at his job, but can be somewhat lacking in delicacy...

Knight of the Ice

Kokoro's Staff

Kenzo Dominic Takiguchi

Kokoro's personal trainer. To find out more, check out *Kiss and Never Cry.*

Hikaru Yomota

Kokoro's assistant coach and a former ice dancer. To find out more, check out *Kiss and Never Cry.*

Takejiro Honda

Kokoro's coach. Masato Tamura, Raito Tamura's grandfather and coach, is his longtime rival.

Moriyama

Kokoro's manager. She's not afraid to get a little pushy if that's what it takes to get results.

Kokoro's Rivals

Fuuta Kumano

He can always rely on his speed and his devilish cuteness. 15 years old.

Raito Tamura

He dazzles the crowd with his passion and expressiveness. 21 years old.

Taiga Aoki

His greatest strength is his ability to land two different quad jumps. 19 years old.

Lilika

An avid fan of Kokoro's.

Kokoro's Family

Maria & Anna Kijinami

Kokoro's younger twin sisters.

Kokoro's Father

President of the Kijinami Group, a company that runs a number of boutique ryokan.

Contents

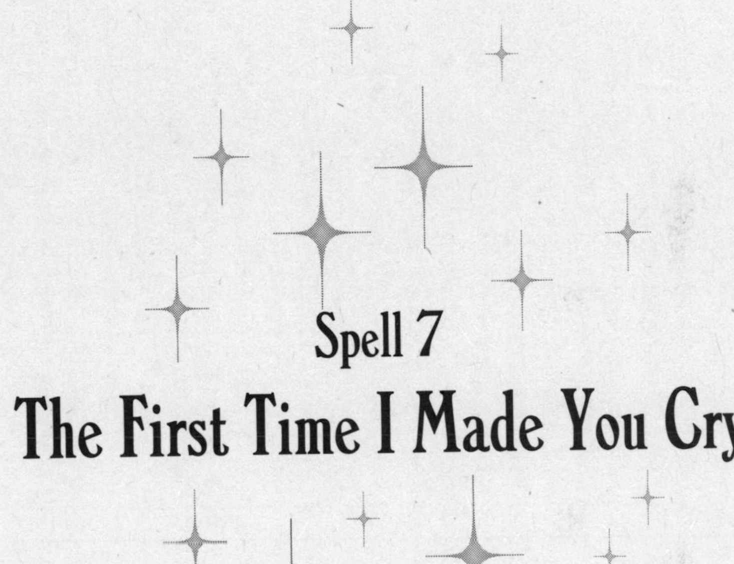

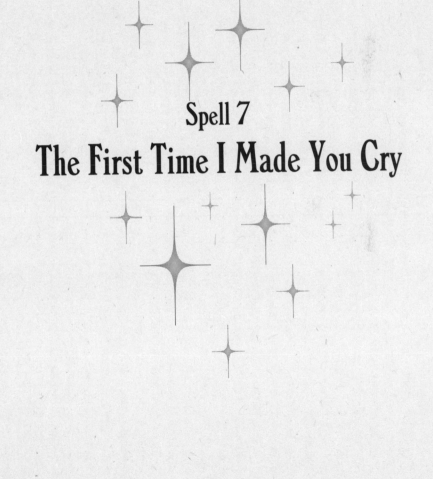

Spell 7
The First Time I Made You Cry

AAAGH... I'VE DONE IT AGAIN.

I HAVEN'T CHANGED SINCE WE WERE KIDS.

I GET MAD AT MYSELF, TAKE IT OUT ON SE-CHAN, AND THEN TURN TAIL.

SHE ALWAYS REACTED THE SAME WAY.

ANY SECOND NOW.

SHE'S GONNA COME RUNNIN' UP, AND...

SWIP
くるっ

SNIFFLE
SWHP
とぼ
SWHP
とぼ
SWHP
とぼ...

MY PRINCE...?! HE'S...!
DASH

SE-CHAN...

AIN'TCHA GONNA DROP KICK ME?

NUH-UH...

HOW 'BOUT A HEAD-BUTT?

YOU'RE TOO DANG TALL, KOKOPPE.

I CAN'T REACH.

PFFT!

DO YA GOTTA LAUGH?

OH, YEAH...
I GUESS THINGS AREN'T THE SAME AS WHEN WE WERE KIDS...

BONK

BADUMP

SORRY... ABOUT THAT...

...IT'S FINE...

OH, NO...
WHAT IF SHE'S THE REASON HE'S HAVING PROBLEMS?
WELL, I WON'T LET HER GET AWAY WITH IT! WHO IS SHE, ANYWAY?!

Kodan Publishing
AND NOW, THE NATIONAL FIGURE SKATING CHAMPIONSHIPS ARE ONLY A WEEK AWAY!
IN WOMEN'S FIGURE SKATING, ALL EYES ARE ON MAYO ASAMA, WITH FANS EXPECTING YET ANOTHER VICTORY FOR HER.

Pre-National Championships Special Analysis of Japan's Men's Figure Skaters
MEANWHILE, THE COMPETITION IS GETTING HEATED IN THE MEN'S DIVISION!
Raito Tamura (21)
Kokoro Kijinami (21)
Taiga Aoki (19)
AFTER DENSUKE TANAHASHI'S RETIREMENT LAST SEASON, EVERYONE'S EAGER TO SEE WHO WILL TAKE HIS PLACE AS JAPAN'S NEW TOP MEN'S FIGURE SKATER.

ONE MAN STANDS OUT AS THE MOST HOPEFUL CANDIDATE–
KOKORO KIJINAMI!
ALTHOUGH HE COULDN'T QUITE MAKE IT TO THE WINNER'S PODIUM AT THE ISU GRAND PRIX FINAL...
WOW, KOKORO-KUN IS SO HOT!
HE IS HANDSOME, BUT WHAT I REALLY LOVE IS HIS COOL PERSONALITY.
GOD, A NORMAL GIRL WOULD NEVER HAVE A CHANCE WITH HIM.
YOU DON'T KNOW WHAT AN OTAKU HE IS...
YOU'RE SELLIN' YOURSELF SHORT.
Moriyama-san
Urgent
Emergency meeting
Reply
OH.
IT'S A TEXT FROM MORIYAMA-SAN...
"EMERGENCY MEETING"?
I WONDER WHAT'S GOIN' ON...
ASAO
SKATE CENTER

SSHK

YOU WON'T MAKE LEVEL FOUR IF YOU...
THUD
THUD
THUD

OKAY, STOP RIGHT THERE.
THAT WAS IT.
WHEN YOU DO THE ROCKER TURN AT THE END OF THAT ONE-FOOT AXEL, YOU NEED TO SHIFT YOUR WEIGHT TO YOUR INSIDE EDGE SOONER.

STOMP

FWUGH!

WHAM

THUD

THUD

THUD

IT HASN'T TAKEN LONG FOR RUMORS TO SPREAD OVER THE INTERNET. WE'VE GOT A REAL TRASH FIRE ON OUR HANDS.
WE CAN'T LET THE IDEA THAT A WOMAN IS CAUSING KIJINAMI'S PROBLEMS GO UNCHECKED.

ARSON? WHAT BRUTES...
SHE DOESN'T MEAN AN *ACTUAL* TRASH FIRE, COACH.

THERE *IS* ONE SILVER LINING. THE OP MUST'VE BEEN AFRAID TO POST A PHOTO.
ALL THEY SHARED WAS A DRAWING,
WHICH, BY THE WAY, IS THE HIGHEST TRENDING IMAGE ON TWITTER RIGHT NOW.
WH-WHAT *KIND* OF DRAWING...?

TAKE A LOOK.

Prince Kokoro

Strange Woman

Hair in bun

Tiny

Short limbs

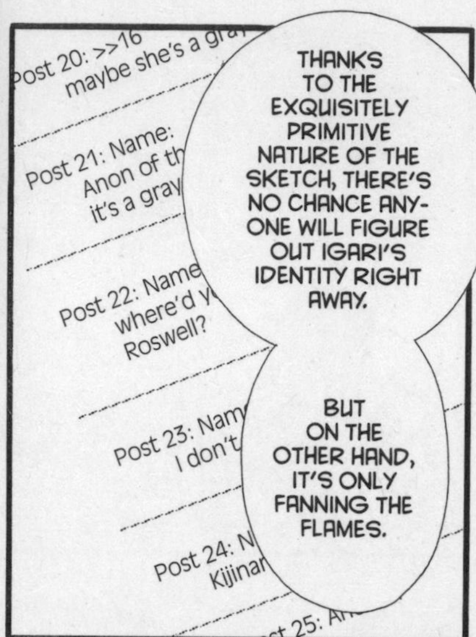
Post 20: >>16
maybe she's a gra
Post 21: Name:
Anon of th
it's a gray
Post 22: Name
where'd y
Roswell?
Post 23: Nam
I don't
Post 24: N
Kijinar
ost 25: An
THANKS TO THE EXQUISITELY PRIMITIVE NATURE OF THE SKETCH, THERE'S NO CHANCE ANY-ONE WILL FIGURE OUT IGARI'S IDENTITY RIGHT AWAY.
BUT ON THE OTHER HAND, IT'S ONLY FANNING THE FLAMES.

HOW COULD IT NOT?
THEY WORSHIP AT KIJINAMI'S FEET LIKE HE'S SOME KIND OF PRINCE.
IT WOULD BE ONE THING TO CATCH HIM EATING OUT OF THE PALM OF SOME STUNNING BEAUTY, BUT A LOONEY TUNE LIKE THIS?

BUT SE-CHAN DOESN'T LOOK ANY-THING LIKE—
SHUT YOUR TRAP!
THIS COULD DESTROY YOUR PUBLIC IMAGE IF WE DON'T DO SOME-THING!
DO YOU *WANT* TO HAVE TO EXPLAIN THIS TO YOUR SPON-SORS?!

FOR NOW, YOU TWO ARE TO STAY AWAY FROM EACH OTHER. UNDER-STOOD?
Anon of the Ice
nami must've lost hi
Anon of the Ice
26: Name: Anon of the Ice
creepy lol
Post 27: Name: Anon of the Ice
I wouldn't mind if she was hot
Name: Anon of the Ice
he's hot for a gra

"HEY, GUESS WHAT I HEARD! KOKORO LIKES SE!"
"NO WAY! YOU MEAN CHITOSE?"
"THAT BOY'S GOT WEIRD TASTE!"

"IT AIN'T LIKE THERE'S A LACK OF GIRLS IN HIS LEAGUE TO CHOOSE FROM."

OH, DON'T ACT LIKE IT'S THE END OF THE WORLD.

IT'S JUST A HANDFUL OF TROLLS CAUSING PROBLEMS. THINGS'LL SETTLE DOWN ONCE THEY GET BORED.

BUT I'M SAD...!
THIS COULD HURT KOKOPPE'S REPUTATION, AND IT'S ALL 'CAUSE OF ME...
HE'LL BE FINE.
HARDCORE RICE CRACKERS

OGATA-SENSEI, I'M DONE FILLING IN THE BLACKS.

BUT... THE NATIONAL CHAMPIONSHIPS ARE COMIN' UP, AND I'M NOT EVEN GONNA BE ABLE TO CAST THE SPELL FOR HIM...

YEAH, THAT SOUNDS LIKE THE BIGGER ISSUE.

BUT HE SAID IT WOULD BE OKAY, DIDN'T HE?

I MEAN, YEAH... BUT YOU REMEMBER WHAT HAPPENED LAST TIME?

EVEN HIS MANAGER SEEMED WORRIED.

SENSEI, SHOULD I PUT A SCREENTONE ON THESE NIPPLES?

AGH...

I'M GONNA HAVE TO HOPE FOR A COFFRET HEART MIRACLE, I GUESS...

HUH? A COFF-WHAT?

OH, SORRY.

YOU KNOW, FROM *LADY LALA*. IT'S LIKE THEIR ULTIMATE ATTACK.

OH, I WOULDN'T KNOW. I'M A MAMI STAN ALL THE WAY.

YATCHAN, HOW OLD *ARE* YOU?

ANYWAY, TELL ME ABOUT THIS ULTIMATE ATTACK.

JUST SOMETHIN' THAT CAME TO MIND.

OH, FORGET IT.

HUH... WELL, I NEED TO GO NOW. BYE.

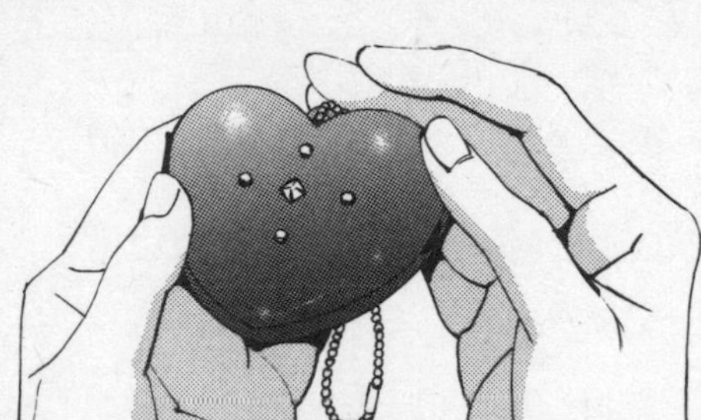

I THINK I CAN POP THIS HEART ON THE END OF MY WAND OPEN.

You can see where it comes apart!

AAACK! DON'T OPEN THAT, PEGA!

AWESOME! OPEN UP, DANG IT!
AAACK! NO, THAT'S WHY YOU CAN'T OPEN IT, PEGA!
IF YOU DO, YOU'LL JUST BREAK IT AND LOSE ALL THE HEART POWER YOU'VE SAVED UP, PEGA!

IT'S LIKE MONEY. YOU HAVE TO SAVE IT BIT BY BIT, PEGA.
BOOORING! WHAT KIND OF MAGICAL BEING ARE YOU?
CHITOSE, KOKORO-KUN HEARD YOU WERE SICK AND CAME TO VISIT.

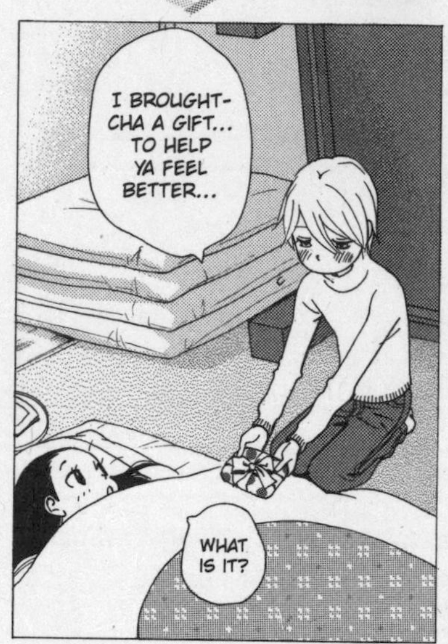
I BROUGHT-CHA A GIFT... TO HELP YA FEEL BETTER...
WHAT IS IT?

OH MY GOSH!
A COFFRET HEART KEY-CHAIN!

I WONDER IF THERE'S SOMETHIN' INSIDE.
UH!
HOLD OFF ON THAT...

Lala

SE-CHAN...

I WONDER IF YOU'RE STILL HOLDIN' ON TO THAT THING, UNOPENED...

KIJINAMI
I'M GETTING WORRIED, MORIYAMA-SAN.
I KNOW YOU'RE GOOD AT WHAT YOU DO, WHICH IS WHY I TRUST YOU WITH MY SON.

SO, I NEED YOU TO TAKE CARE OF THESE NASTY RUMORS BEFORE THEY SPREAD ANY FURTHER.
OF COURSE, SIR.

YOU CAN REST ASSURED...
NOT ONLY WILL YOUR SON'S REPUTATION BE REPAIRED, BUT HE'S GOING TO GET HIS FIRST WIN AT THE NATIONAL CHAMPION-SHIPS.
SEE, I THOUGHT OF A WAY TO KILL TWO BIRDS WITH ONE STONE...

DING DOOONG
DING DOOONG
NGH...

DING DONG
DRAG DRAG
DING DOOONG
WHAT'S GOIN' ON? IT'S TOO EARLY FOR THIS...
GEEZ...

CHIK CHIK
THUNK!!

MO-MORI-YAMA-SAN?
I WANT YOU DOWN-STAIRS AND READY TO GO IN TEN MINUTES!
HUH?!

JUST GET YOUR ASS IN GEAR!
Y-YES, MA'AM!

SO... WHERE ARE WE GOING?
I HAVE A MEETING AT TEN THIS MORNING...
I DON'T WANNA HEAR IT! WE'LL BE DONE WITH YOU BY THEN.

READ THIS OVER.
WH-WHAT IS IT...?

IT'S A BIO FOR CHITOSE IGARI, INSPIRATIONAL TRAINER.

GOOD MORNING.

HEY.

THE NATIONAL FIGURE SKATING CHAMPIONSHIPS START TOMORROW.

YOU'RE HERE EARLIER THAN USUAL, SAWADA-SAN.

YEAH, THE GYM WAS CLOSED FOR RENOVATIONS.

IN THIS SEGMENT, WE'LL INTRODUCE SOME OF THE PROFESSIONALS WHO SUPPORT OUR STAR SKATERS BEHIND THE SCENES.

LET'S TURN TO THE MAN EXPECTED TO WIN FOR THE FIRST TIME AT THIS YEAR'S NATIONAL CHAMPIONSHIPS.

INSPIRATIONAL TRAINER
CHITOSE IGARI (23)
THIS IS CHITOSE IGARI-SAN, INSPIRATIONAL TRAINER!
PFFFT!

IGARI-SAN, YOU'RE 23 YEARS OLD AND HAVE ONLY BEEN OUT OF SCHOOL FOR 2 YEARS.
BUT EVEN AT YOUR YOUNG AGE, WE'RE TOLD YOU'RE AN OUTSTANDING TRAINER.
OH, UHH... WELL, I GUESS YOU COULD SAY THAT...

WHAT THE HELL IS SHE TRYING TO PULL?!
IGA-RIII!

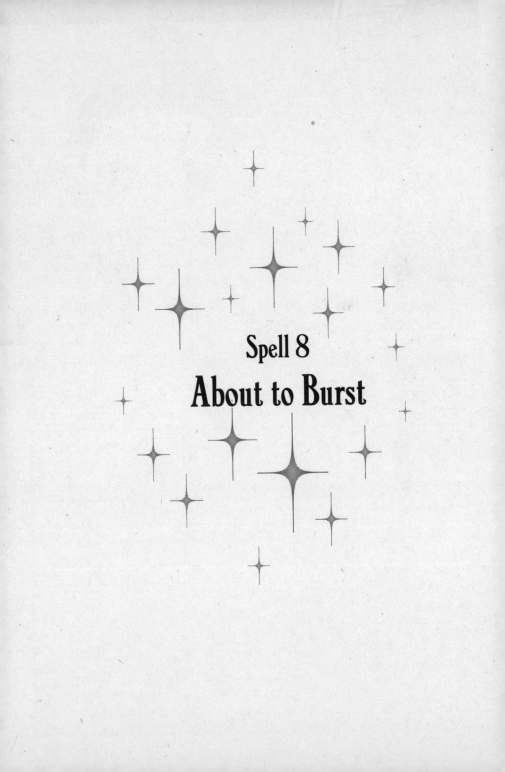

Spell 8
About to Burst

SO...
Kodan Publishing
THIS MORNING'S INCIDENT WAS A ONE-TIME FAVOR FOR A FRIEND IN NEED...

...AND THERE'S NO RISK THAT IT WILL INTERFERE WITH YOUR WORK GOING FORWARD.
IS THAT CORRECT?
...YES, SIR.
HEY.
FWICK
LOOK ME IN THE EYE WHEN YOU ANSWER ME.

TH—
THAT'S RIGHT...
BOSS.

...

WELL, IN THAT CASE, A STRICT WARNING SHOULD SUFFICE FOR NOW...
HOW-EVER...
AS I'M SURE YOU'RE AWARE, COMPANY POLICY CLEARLY FORBIDS EMPLOYEES FROM TAKING ON SIDE JOBS.

SHOULD YOU TAKE A PAYCHECK FROM ANY THIRD PARTIES, OR WORSE, APPEAR ON TV AND EXPOSE YOUR FACE TO THE PUBLIC LIKE YOU DID TODAY...
...BE AWARE THAT I MAY HAVE TO TAKE HARSHER MEASURES.
HEY, SO DOES THIS MEAN IGA-CHAN* KNOWS KOKORO KIJINAMI?
SHH!
HONESTLY, I CAN'T BELIEVE YOU WOULD GO BEHIND MY BACK AND—

*IGA-CHAN IS A CUTESY NICKNAME FOR CHITOSE.

HOW DO THEY EVEN KNOW EACH OTHER? THINK WE CAN GET HIS AUTOGRAPH?

HOW SHOULD I KNOW?!

HEY! QUIT EAVES-DROPPING AND GET TO WORK!

YES, SIR!

YES, SIR!

YOU'RE TELLING THEM...
...SE-CHAN'S MY TRAINER?

BRILLIANT IDEA, RIGHT? I JUST KEEP OUTDOING MYSELF. ♡
THIS SHOULD PUT A STOP TO THE RUMORS THAT YOU HAVE SOME SORT OF WEIRD FETISH.
AND NOW, WE DON'T HAVE TO WORRY ABOUT WHAT PEOPLE THINK WHEN WE MAKE HER COME WITH US.

BUT... SHE'S GOT A JOB...
OH, THAT WON'T BE AN ISSUE.
I ALREADY HAVE A PLAN FOR WHEN THE TIME COMES.

MORI-YAMA-SAN.
I... I DON'T NEED NO SPELL TO WIN.
SO, PLEASE... CAN WE STOP CAUSIN' PROBLEMS FOR SE-CHAN—

EX-CUSE ME?

YOU'VE GOT SOME NERVE TO SAY THAT AFTER YOU FELL ON YOUR FACE IN CANADA!
A VIRGIN LIKE YOU HAS NO RIGHT TO ARGUE WITH ME!

I DIDN'T KNOW KOKORO WAS A VIRGIN.
KOKORO'S MANAGER IS ONE SCARY LADY.
DAIKYO
SHE'S JUST CALLING HIM NAMES...
YOU, TOO, KOKORO...?

IGARI-SAN, WE HEAR YOUR BACKGROUND STUDYING PSYCHOLOGY HAS ENABLED YOU TO SUPPORT KIJINAMI'S MENTAL HEALTH.
Figure Skating Behind the Scenes: Direct Interview with an Inspirational Trainer!
Diary
OH... UHH, YES...

AS HIS INSPIRATIONAL TRAINER, IGARI-SAN HAS KIJINAMI'S COMPLETE TRUST, AND USING TECHNIQUES SUCH AS THESE...
Kokoro
HIS TRAINER...?
THAT'S NOT HOW IT LOOKED TO ME, BUT...

IF IT'S TRUE, THEN SHE'S ACTUALLY A CRUCIAL ALLY OF PRINCE KOKORO'S!
I HAVE A RESPONSIBILITY TO CLEAR HER NAME...!

KOSE
WELCOME TO THE NATIONAL FIGURE SKATING CHAMPIONSHIPS!
TODAY, WE'RE BROADCASTING THE MEN'S SHORT PROGRAM.
RAITO ☆
Kijinami
Kokoro
RIGHT NOW, THE SKATERS FROM GROUP FOUR ARE ON THE ICE BEGINNING THEIR WARM-UPS.
OF PARTICULAR NOTE AMONG THIS GROUP IS KOKORO KIJINAMI, WHO WILL BE SKATING LAST AS NUMBER 24.

THIS COMPETITION WILL ALSO DECIDE WHO WILL REPRESENT JAPAN AT THE WORLD CHAMPIONSHIPS NEXT MARCH. ISN'T THAT RIGHT, TANAHASHI-SAN?
THAT'S RIGHT. IT'S ANOTHER REASON THIS IS SUCH A SPECIAL EVENT FOR THE SKATERS HERE TODAY.

I WONDER IF KIJINAMI'S SUPER TRAINER IS HERE TODAY.
OH, I HEARD ABOUT HER! IS IT TRUE, THEN?
PRESS

WORD IS THAT HIS SUDDEN IMPROVEMENT CAME RIGHT AFTER SHE JOINED HIS STAFF.
WOW! SHE MUST REALLY BE GOOD.
SMIRK

THE FIRST SKATER IN THIS GROUP IS THIS YEAR'S JUNIOR CHAMPION, FUUTA KUMANO.

CLAP CLAP CLAP CLAP

WOOOOOO

Fuuta!

You got this!

HE'LL BE SKATING TO THE TUNE OF "LET YOURSELF GO," FROM THE MOVIE "FOLLOW THE FLEET."

HE'S ADDED THE TRIPLE AXEL TO HIS REPERTOIRE THIS SEASON, BUT HE STILL HASN'T LANDED ONE CLEANLY YET.
LET'S SEE IF HE OPENS WITH THIS CHALLENGING JUMP...
THERE'S A DOUBLE AXEL.
HE PLAYED IT SAFE!
HE'S SURE TO GET BONUS POINTS FOR THE MASTERFUL EXECUTION ON THAT JUMP.

HIS SPINS APPEAR TO HAVE ALL OF THE IMPORTANT LEVEL FEATURES.

NOW HERE COMES A TRIPLE FLIP, A TRIPLE LOOP...

...AND A STEP INTO A TRIPLE SALCHOW.

WHOOPS!

HE LOST HIS BALANCE ON THAT STEP!

きゅんっ…
BADUMP
Maternal Instincts

WOW! I GOT SO MANY POINTS!
THAT KID'S GONNA GROW UP TO BE A REAL CON ARTIST...
FUUTA KUMANO'S GREATEST STRENGTH: EMOTIONAL MANIPU-LATION
It won't work on me, though.

IS THAT KIJINAMI'S TRAINER, THE ONE PEOPLE ARE TALKING ABOUT?
HER...?

IT KINDA FEELS LIKE...
...ALL EYES ARE ON ME...

They made her wear a team jersey.
MORIYAMA-SAN SAYS I GOTTA STICK WITH KOKOPPE AT ALL TIMES, NOT JUST WHEN I'M CASTIN' THE SPELL...
BUT GAAAH, ALL I WANT IS A HIDIN' PLACE...

SHF

SMILE

TH-THANK YOU...
CANDY?

GLANCE

HM? WHAT?
OH.
NOTHIN'...

ANYWAY, IT'S ABOUT TIME FOR ME TO GO ON.
OH! YEAH.
GOOD LUCK!

WEIRD... HE SEEMS MORE CONFIDENT THAN USUAL.

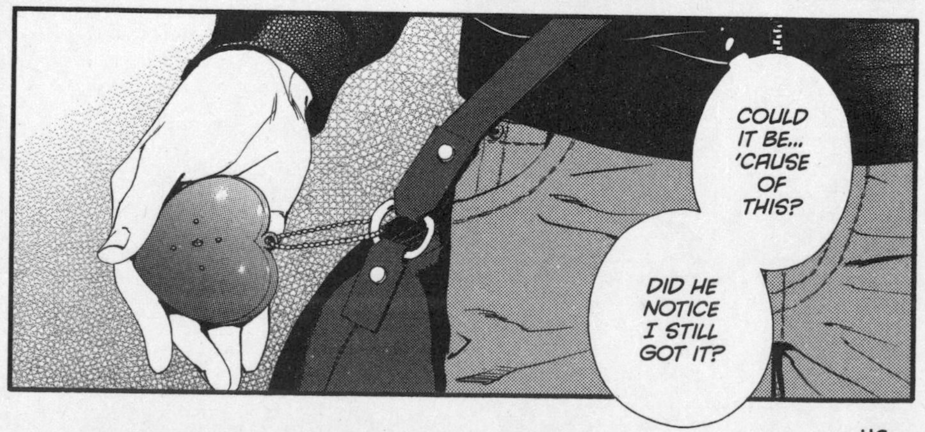
COULD IT BE... 'CAUSE OF THIS?
DID HE NOTICE I STILL GOT IT?

IT'S KINDA EMBARRASSIN', BUT MAYBE I SHOULD TELL HIM WHEN THIS IS OVER...
ABOUT HOW I'VE HELD ON TO IT WITHOUT OPENIN' IT ALL THIS TIME...

ON THE ICE, KOKORO KIJINAMI...
WOOOOO
ACK!
BETTER GET TO MY SEAT!

KIJINAMI IS CONSIDERED THE MOST LIKELY CANDIDATE FOR FIRST PLACE.
KOKORO
KOKORO
KOKORO
DESPITE HIS UNFORTUNATE PERFORMANCE AT THE GRAND PRIX FINAL,

HIS QUADRUPLE JUMPS LOOKED VERY CLEAN WHEN HE WAS PRACTICING EARLIER.
INDEED. AND I EXPECT WE'LL SEE MORE OF THOSE IN A MOMENT.

THOSE ARE THE OPENING NOTES OF "MOONLIGHT SONATA"...

HE'S GOING FOR A QUAD TOE LOOP...
AND HE LANDS IT!
SHUDDER

WHAT'S WITH THIS FEELIN' I'M GETTIN'?
BADUMP
IT'S HARDLY MY FIRST TIME SEEIN' KOKOPPE SKATE...
BADUMP
BUT IT'S LIKE SOMETHIN' IS GROWIN' INSIDE ME...
BADUMP
I FEEL LIKE IT'S GONNA BURST...
BADUMP
AAAH...

PLEASE DON'T LET IT GET ANY BIGGER.

WHAT-EVER IT IS THAT'S TRY-ING TO BURST OUT...

I'M REALLY AFRAID OF IT RIGHT NOW...

WOOOOOOO!
A FLAWLESS PERFORMANCE BY KOKORO KIJINAMI!
THE CROWD'S GIVING HIM A STANDING OVATION!

WOOOOO!
WELL, MARIA, IT LOOKS LIKE OUR BROTHER IS GOING TO WIN AGAIN...
WHY DO YOU SAY THAT LIKE IT'S A BAD THING, ANNA?
WHERE'S THE FUN IF THERE'S NO SUSPENSE?
CLAP
CLAP
CLAP
CLAP
CLAP
CLAP
CLAP
ICE

HEY, DO YOU KNOW WHERE IGARI-CHAN IS?
Kodan Publishing
LAST I HEARD SHE WAS LEAVING FOR A MEETING.

Schedule
OH, YEAH. IT SAYS HERE SHE WENT STRAIGHT HOME AFTER A MEETING WITH OGATA-SAN.
HMM.
I DON'T KNOW. WHAT IF SHE'S ACTUALLY OUT WATCHING FIGURE SKATING?

AREN'T THEY HOLDING THE NATIONAL CHAMPIONSHIPS OR SOMETHING RIGHT NOW?
TURN ON THE TV, BEFORE SAWADA-SAN SHOWS UP.
IT'LL BE SO FUNNY IF WE SAW HER THERE!
AH HA HA!

FWICK
NOW, LET'S HEAR WHAT KIJINAMI HAS TO SAY.
H·S

THAT COMPETITION YOU MENTIONED...

AND THE SCORES HAVE COME IN FOR RAITO TAMURA.

DAITO KYODAI

EEEEKKK!

Raito-kun! ♡

IT LOOKS LIKE HE COULDN'T CATCH UP TO KIJINAMI, BUT HE SEEMS SATISFIED TO HAVE BEATEN HIS PERSONAL BEST.

AND WHILE HE CAN'T PERFORM ANY QUAD JUMPS,
HE PICKED UP QUITE A FEW BONUS POINTS WITH FLOURISHES LIKE RAISING HIS HANDS IN MID-AIR AND WEAVING STEPS IN BETWEEN HIS JUMPS.
I SEE!
HOW TOUCHING THAT THE BOY FINALLY LEARNED TO DO TRIPLE AXELS.
HE CAN SPEAK UP IF IT'S TO MAKE COACH TAMURA MAD...

WOOOO
OUR NEXT SKATER IS ANOTHER CANDIDATE FOR FIRST PLACE.
ON THE ICE, REPRESENTING DAIKYO UNIVERSITY, TAIGA AOKI.
AOKI WILL PERFORM HIS SHORT PROGRAM TO THE TUNE OF "DANSE MACABRE."
HE WAS UNABLE TO ADVANCE TO THE GRAND PRIX FINAL AFTER A SPRAIN FORCED HIM TO WITHDRAW FROM THE NHK TROPHY JUST BEFORE THE FREE SKATE,
BUT YOU CAN ALWAYS COUNT ON HIM TO BRING POWER TO HIS JUMPS.
YES, AND HE'LL BE GOING INTO THE FREE SKATE READY TO PERFORM TWO DIFFERENT KINDS OF QUADS.

THERE'S A QUAD TOE LOOP...
...AND A TRIPLE TOE LOOP!
HE NAILED THE COMBO!
I AIN'T NEVER SEEN *HIM* BEFORE! THAT WAS SO COOL!
HE STILL AIN'T AS COOL AS OUR BROTHER!
HE PULLS OFF A TRIPLE AXEL.
NEXT, HE'S GOING FOR A STEP, FOLLOWED BY A TRIPLE FLIP...

Apparently, their accents come out when they're excited.

WAIT, WHAT'S THIS?
HUH ?!
A QUADRUPLE SALCHOW, LADIES AND GENTLEMEN!
WOOOOO!
THAT'S THE SECOND QUAD JUMP IN AOKI'S SHORT PROGRAM!

THAT'S ALL THE REQUIRED JUMPS!
AND THIS ROCK MIX SOUNDS ALL THE MORE INTENSE WITH THE CROWD'S APPLAUSE!
WOOO OOOOO!
AN ASTOUNDING PERFORMANCE BY TAIGA AOKI!
THE CROWD IS GIVING HIM A STANDING OVATION!
LET'S SEE THE SCORE...
WOW! A TECHNICAL SCORE OF 48.25!
HIS PROGRAM COMPONENTS SCORE WASN'T QUITE AS HIGH AS KIJINAMI'S, BUT HE JUST BARELY MANAGED TO COME OUT ON TOP!

MORIYAMA-SAN WAS MAKING A FACE LIKE YOU WOULDN'T BELIEVE.

WOO HOO! THAT'S WHAT I'M TALKIN' ABOUT!
ANNA! I'MMA TELL DADDY ON YOU!

BUT I NOTICED SOME-THING...

KOKOPPE SEEMED TO HAVE THIS LIGHT IN HIS EYES LIKE I'D NEVER SEEN BEFORE.

Knight of the ICE

Knight of the Ice The story so far

She may be small, but she's our heroine!
TEN HUT!

CHITOSE IS AN EDITOR FOR A HEALTH-AND-LIFESTYLE MAGAZINE AT A SMALL PUBLISHING COMPANY.

AND CHITOSE'S CHILDHOOD FRIEND, KOKORO, IS A STAR FIGURE SKATER!

IT TURNS OUT KOKORO PERFORMS MORE CONSISTENTLY WHEN CHITOSE CASTS A SPELL FOR HIM, SO NOW SHE HAS TO GO TO ALL HIS COMPETITIONS...

He made it to the Grand Prix Final! Yay!
My first cover story! Yay!
...they're at the same time.
But...

BUT THEN, CHITOSE HAS A SCHEDULING CONFLICT BETWEEN HER OVERSEAS BUSINESS TRIP AND AN IMPORTANT COMPETITION.

I'LL GIVE IT MY ALL, EVEN WITHOUT YOU THERE, SE-CHAN.
Yes, he has eyes.

HEARING THAT, CHITOSE LEAVES FOR HER BUSINESS TRIP WITH PEACE OF MIND, AND KOKORO TRIES TO SHOW HER WHAT HE'S CAPABLE OF...

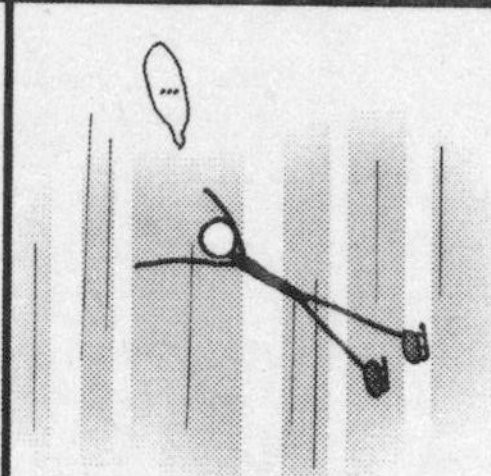

...BUT HE SUFFERS AN AGONIZING DEFEAT AFTER LOSING HIS FOCUS WHEN HE FINDS OUT CHITOSE IS BEING ACCOMPANIED ABROAD BY HER HANDSOME BOSS.

BACK IN JAPAN, THEIR COMPLICATED FEELINGS LEAD TO CONFLICT, AND A DIEHARD FAN OF KOKORO'S SEES IT HAPPEN.

QUIT ACTIN' LIKE YOU'RE MY MOTHER!
Why is he mad?!
What a suspicious woman...
That's you.

THE RESEMBLANCE IS PERFECT, LOL.

THAT'S WHEN RUMORS BEGIN TO SPREAD ONLINE THAT CHITOSE IS STALKING KOKORO AND IS THE REASON FOR HIS TROUBLES.

TO PREEMPT ANY DAMAGE TO KOKORO'S REPUTATION, HIS MANAGER GETS THE NEWS TO REPORT THAT CHITOSE IS HIS TALENTED TRAINER.

...for teen virgin pride!

My 4T...

AND AMID ALL THAT, THE NATIONAL FIGURE SKATING CHAMPIONSHIPS BEGIN. KOKORO EXECUTES HIS SHORT PROGRAM FLAWLESSLY, BUT HIS RIVAL TAIGA STEALS AHEAD BY PERFORMING AN UNBELIEVABLE TWO QUADRUPLE JUMPS IN ONE PROGRAM!

story ← tinues

These drawings are purely symbolic. Parts may differ from the actual story, so please view them alongside volume 1, on sale now. ♡

Yayoi Ogawa

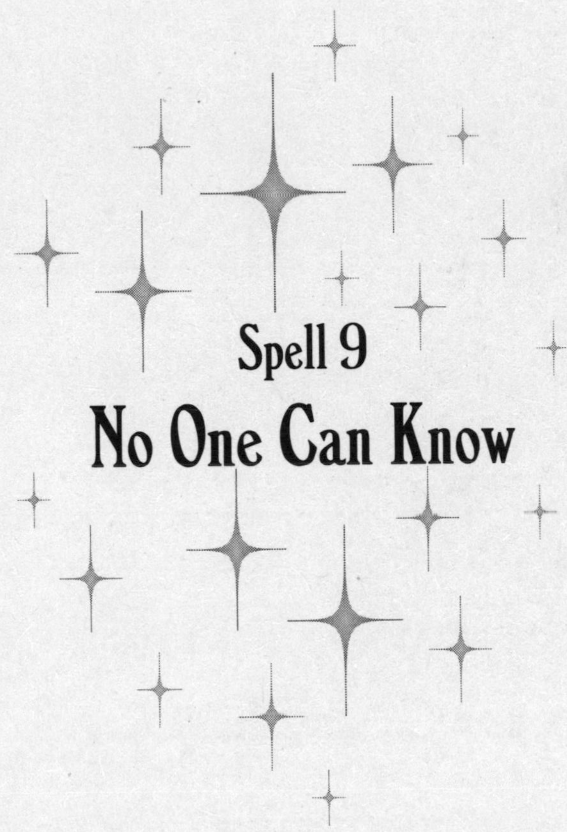

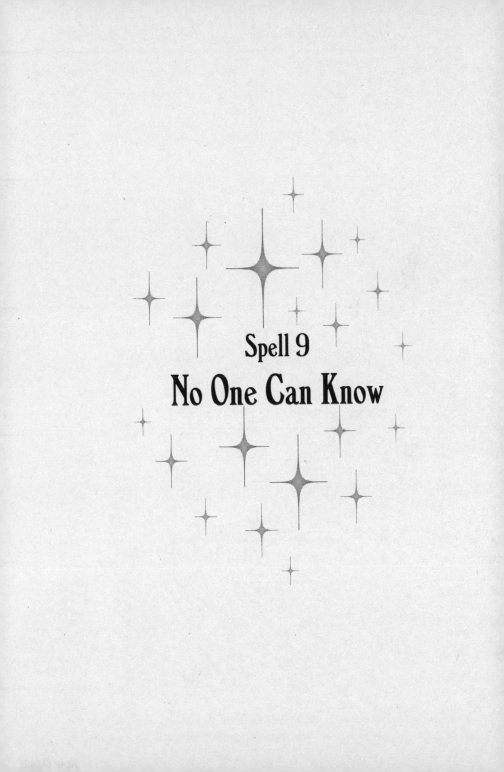

Spell 9
No One Can Know

KOKOPPE MOVED AWAY TO TRAIN ABROAD RIGHT AFTER STARTING HIGH SCHOOL.
WHENEVER I SENT AN EMAIL ASKING HOW HE WAS DOING, HE'D ALWAYS REPLY.

BUT HE ONLY INITIATED ONCE.
HE SENT ME A SHORT VIDEO, NOT EVEN TEN SECONDS LONG.

THE DESCRIPTION READ, "NO ONE ELSE CAN KNOW ABOUT THIS."
YAHOO! YOU DID IT!
I WAS SHOCKED AT WHAT I SAW WHEN I WATCHED IT...

...BUT I WON'T TELL THAT STORY JUST YET.
FIRST...
HEY, MEATBALL HEAD!

COME WITH ME! MOVE IT!
WHAAAT?!
I CAN'T. I'M NOT EVEN DRESSED...
Besides, aren'tcha cold, Moriyama-san?

OH, YEAH. I GUESS YOU SHOULD PUT ON SOME PANTIES.
AND A FEW OTHER THINGS!
Ya mind not peekin'?!

IS KOKOP— I MEAN— KOKORO-KUN HAVING SOME KIND OF PROBLEM?
HE'S IN A TEAM MEETING ABOUT THE SHORT PROGRAM AND HOW TO APPROACH THE FREE SKATE.
BUT FOR SOME REASON, COACH HONDA CAN'T GET THROUGH TO HIM.

OHHH... YEAH, I GUESS TAIGA-KUN BEAT HIM BY LANDING THOSE TWO QUADS...
BUT I RECKON KOKOPPE CAN MAKE UP FOR THAT IN THE FREE SKATE...

WAIT...

YOU MEAN...
...YOU WANNA INCLUDE TWO QUADS IN YOUR FREE SKATE?

KOKORO, YOU STILL HAVE THE HIGHER PRESENTATION SCORE.
YOUR BEST SHOT AT WINNING IS A PERFECT FREE SKATE WITH THE PROGRAM WE PLANNED ON.

THE ONLY QUAD YOU CAN DO IS A 4T*. ONE OF THEM WOULD HAVE TO BE A COMBO.
IF YOU CHANGE YOUR PROGRAM AND MESS IT UP, WE'RE GOING TO HAVE ANOTHER DISASTER ON OUR HANDS.

*4T = QUADRUPLE TOE LOOP

IT WOULD BE ONE THING IF THIS WAS SOMETHING YOU'D BEEN PRACTICING, BUT THERE'S NO WAY YOU CAN JUST PULL IT OUT OF YOUR ASS AT NATIONALS.
HAVE YOU FORGOT-TEN WHAT HAPPENED IN CANADA?
YOU'RE TALK-ING NON-SENSE.

...IT'LL BE FINE.
I'M DOING TWO QUADS.

OOF...
THIS ISN'T LOOKIN' GOOD...

KOKOPPE GETS AWFUL COMBATIVE WHEN HIS EARS TURN RED AND HE STARTS GRINDIN' HIS TEETH LIKE THAT.
ANYTHING YOU TRY TO TELL HIM IS JUST GONNA MAKE HIM MORE STUBBORN...
She can tell by the way his jaw moves.

I'M PROBABLY THE ONLY ONE HERE WHO KNOWS HOW TO HANDLE THIS...
AW, HECK...
Are you even listen-ing?!

WELL, HEY!
WHY DON'TCHA GO AHEAD AND TRY IT?

I KNOW YA CAN DO IT, KOKOPPE!
WHO NEEDS PRACTICE? TWO QUADS AIN'T NOTHIN'!

WAIT, WH—
SHH!

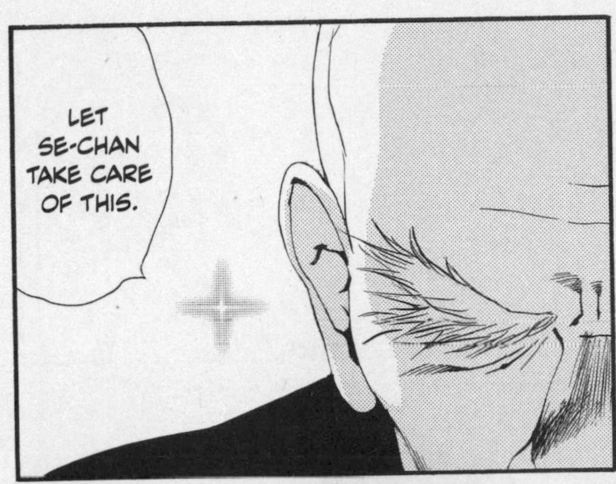
LET SE-CHAN TAKE CARE OF THIS.

LET'S SEE WHAT YOU CAN DO, MEATBALL HEAD.

OHHH, I CAN'T WAIT TO SEE YA WIN TOMORROW, KOKOPPE!
MEETING'S OVER, EVERY-BODY!
U-UMM...

OH! THAT REMINDS ME.
DON'TCHA HAVE THAT *SPECIAL MOVE,* KOKOPPE?
FLINCH

SPECIAL MOVE?

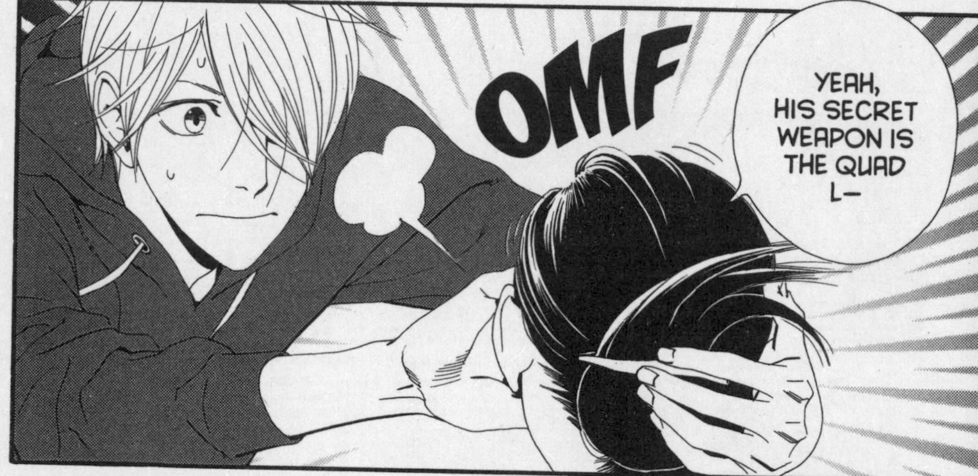
YEAH, HIS SECRET WEAPON IS THE QUAD L—
OMF

COME HERE, SE-CHAN.
MMF MMF MMF!

CLICK!
HUSH...

SE-CHAN, I TOLD YOU...
YEAH, "NO ONE ELSE CAN KNOW." SO YA WANT ME TO SHUT UP ABOUT IT?
DON'TCHA WANNA WIN?

I WAS JUST PLAYIN' AROUND AND GOT LUCKY WHEN I LANDED THAT.
I'M NOT GOOD ENOUGH TO INCLUDE IT IN MY PROGRAM...
BUT YOU'RE GOOD ENOUGH AT QUAD TOE LOOPS? YOU'VE DONE TWO OF *THOSE* BEFORE...

I MEAN... I'VE TRIED IT IN PRACTICE...
YOU'VE TRIED IT?
SO, YA MEAN YOU'VE ALREADY BEEN PRACTICIN' THE MODIFIED PROGRAM?

...

...KO-KOPPE.

I...WANNA SEE YOU STANDIN' UP IN THE CENTER OF THE WINNERS' PODIUM TOMORROW.

JUST DO WHATCHA GOTTA DO TO MAKE THAT HAPPEN.

THAT VIDEO KOKOPPE SENT ME FOUR YEARS AGO WAS OF HIM DURING PRACTICE.
HE LANDED AN EX-TREMELY DIFFICULT JUMP: THE QUAD LUTZ.
YAHOO! YOU DID IT!

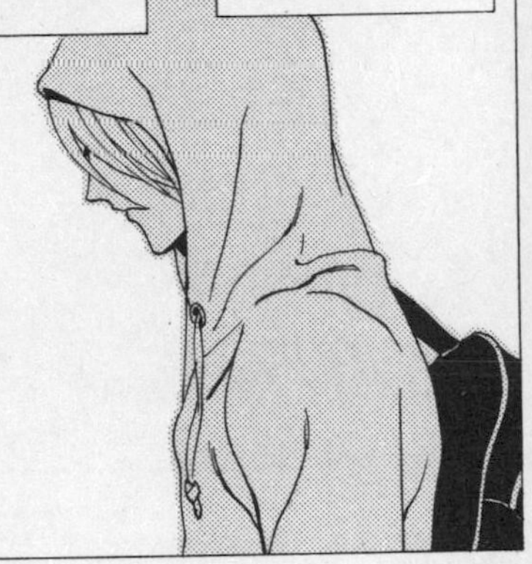
HIS PERFORMANCE WOULD GO ON TO SUFFER DUE TO A TRAINING INJURY, THOUGH.

HE ENDED UP GOING TO COLLEGE IN TOKYO AND STARTED PRACTICING AT HIS CURRENT RINK.

MEANWHILE, I HAD QUIT SKATING AND WAS GOING TO COLLEGE IN SENDAI.
AT SOME POINT, I REALIZED WE'D FALLEN OUT OF TOUCH.

BUT THEN LAST SUM-MER...
...WE MET AGAIN.

THE NEXT DAY...
WOOOOO
MEN'S FREE SKATE, FINAL GROUP WARM-UPS
LOOKS LIKE A TOSS-UP BETWEEN AOKI AND KIJINAMI FOR FIRST.
I GUESS THEY'RE BOTH STANDING THEIR GROUND.
I DON'T SEE ANY MAJOR REVISIONS TO THEIR PLANNED PROGRAM COMPONENTS.
MOST OF AOKI'S POINTS WILL COME FROM THE QUAD TOE LOOPS AND SALCHOWS HE OPENS WITH.
PLUS, HIS TRIPLE AXEL-DOUBLE TOE LOOP-DOUBLE LOOP COMBO TOWARDS THE END.
ON THE OTHER HAND, KIJINAMI'S GOING TO BEGIN WITH A QUAD TOE LOOP.
THEN, IN THE LATTER HALF, IT LOOKS LIKE HE'LL DO A TRIPLE AXEL-TRIPLE TOE LOOP COMBO AND ANOTHER 3-3 COMBO WITH A LUTZ AND A TOE LOOP.
SO, WITH THAT LUTZ COMBO IN THERE, HIS BASE SCORE WILL BE HIGHER THAN IT WAS AT THE FINAL.

YEAH, I SAW HIM RAISING HIS HANDS AS HE JUMPED WHEN HE WAS PRACTIC-ING IT THIS MORNING.
HE'LL GET A LOT OF BONUS POINTS IF HE CAN PULL THAT OFF. AND SINCE IT'S IN THE SECOND HALF, EVERYTHING'S BASE VALUE IS MULTIPLIED BY A FACTOR OF 1.1.
PRES

IT LOOKS LIKE AOKI IS GOING TO SKATE THIRD AND KIJINAMI IS GOING TO SKATE LAST.
RAITO
Kokoro
mi
WOW, MY HEART'S RACING!

MEANWHILE, RAITO WAS STILL IN HIS OWN LITTLE WORLD.
...FIVE, SIX, SEVEN.
I'm the star of the show!
NICE! MY FANS BROUGHT ONE MORE BANNER THAN KOKORO'S! ♪
Heh.
COME ON! SHOW ME THAT UPRIGHT SPIN!

...UH-OH.

!
WOO!
FLINCH
びくっ

Ice Rink
I GOT FIVE MISSED CALLS FROM MY BOSS...
I DON'T THINK I CAN KEEP IGNORIN' HIM MUCH LONGER...

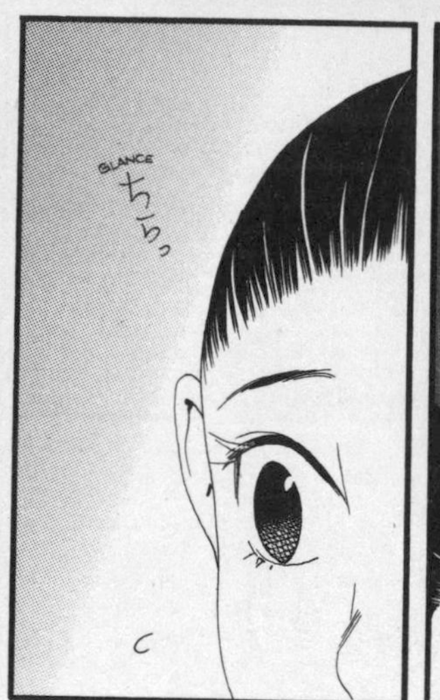
GLANCE
ちらっ

CLAP
CLAP
CLAP
CLAP
THAT'S TAIGA-KUN'S SONG...
HE MUSTA LANDED SOMETHIN' REALLY FANCY...

I WONDER... IS HE HEARIN' THIS...?

KO-KOPPE.
WANT ME TO CAST THE SPELL NOW?

EXCUSE ME, COACH.
NOD コク

TA-DA!

WOOOOO!
THAT WAS TAIGA AOKI! HE DIDN'T MAKE ANY MISTAKES, ASIDE FROM THAT IFFY LANDING ON HIS FIRST QUAD JUMP.
YOU COULD TELL HE WAS TIRED BY THE SECOND HALF, BUT HE KEPT GOING UNTIL THE VERY END.
CLAP
CLAP
CLAP

WOOOO!
HIS TOTAL SCORE IS 238.14.
THAT'S THE HIGHEST WE'VE SEEN TODAY BY FAR!

"ROC SOL, ROC SOL, POLLY POLLY MIRACULUM."

"O, MY KNIGHT..."
"LET YOUR TRUE STRENGTH BE RESTORED!"

IS THAT THE COFFRET HEART I GAVE YA?

KIJINAMI
OH! YEAH.
THIS IS IT. I DIDN'T HAVE IT OUT LIKE THIS, BUT I'VE BEEN HOLDIN' ON TO IT THIS WHOLE TIME...

HAVE YOU OPENED IT?
BA DUMP

HUH?
KIJI-NAMI!
He's right in my face...

YOU'RE UP.
UH, YES!
HAVE YOU DONE YOUR BUSI-NESS?

SE-CHAN.
I'M GONNA WIN THIS.

ACK!
THERE I GO AGAIN...
BADUMP!

UGH, I CAN'T TAKE IT...
WHY IS THIS HAPPENIN'...?
BA-DUMP
BA-DUMP
BA-DUMP
GOOD JOB, MEATBALL HEAD. LOOKS LIKE YOU'VE GOT A HANDLE ON HIM.

HUH?
YOU REALLY KNOW HOW TO CONTROL HIS THINK-ING.
THAT'S A USEFUL SKILL FOR HIS "PERSONAL TRAINER."

ACTUALLY, ABOUT THAT. I DON'T THINK I CAN DO IT.
MY JOB WON'T REALLY ALLOW ME TO PLAY A PUBLIC ROLE...
Besides, it's not like I know how to plan a training regimen...
OH? IT SEEMS LIKE A GOOD OPPORTUNITY FOR YOU, IN MY OPINION.

THINK ABOUT IT.
YOU CAN SPEND ALL YOUR TIME HANGING OFF THE ARM OF YOUR BELOVED KOKOPPE. ♡
BOING
びよん

WH-WH-WHUH?
WHAT'S GOT YOU ALL TONGUE-TIED?
IT'S NOT HARD TO TELL YOU HAVE FEELINGS FOR HIM.

WH-WH-WHAT DO YOU MEAN, FEEL-INGS...?!

IT AIN'T LIKE THERE'S A LACK OF GIRLS IN HIS LEAGUE TO CHOOSE FROM.

I WOULDN'T MIND IF SHE WAS HOT, BUT DAMN...

KIJINAMI MUST'VE LOST HIS MIND LOL

I DON'T HAVE FEEL-INGS FOR KOKOPPE...!

YOU DON'T HAVE TO HIDE IT.
I-I'M NOT HIDING ANY-THING!
HE'S STARTIN'.
I GOT-TA GO WATCH...!
HEY! I'M NOT DONE WITH YOU.
CLACK
HE'S OPENING WITH A QUAD TOE LOOP.
OH, NO. ACTUALLY...

"KOKOPPE."
"I WANNA SEE YOU STANDIN' UP IN THE CENTER OF THE WINNERS' PODIUM."

WHEN THEY'RE PERFECTLY SYNCHRONIZED, IT RELEASES ALL ITS HEART POWER...
...AND PEGASUS KNIGHT CAN CHANGE INTO HIS FINAL FORM: SUPREME WING!
CLAAANG!

IT'S A TRIPLE-
SCRATCH THAT...
A QUAD-
RUPLE...
...LUTZ!

WHOOOOA!

A LUTZ... REALLY?!
YES.
HIS HAND DID LIGHTLY TOUCH THE ICE, BUT IT LOOKED LIKE HE GOT THE ROTATIONS IN.

VERY FEW SKATERS HAVE EVER LANDED A QUAD LUTZ AT A SANCTIONED COMPETITION, BUT KIJINAMI WENT FOR IT!
THE BASE VALUE IS 3.3 POINTS HIGHER THAN A TOE LOOP!
I almost had a heart attack!
OH MY GOD...

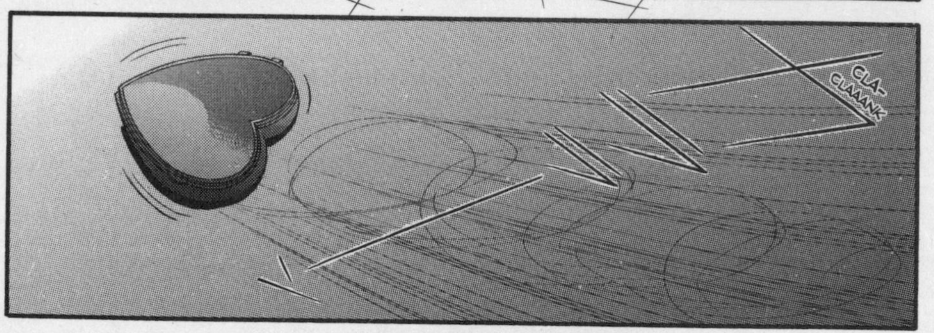
CLA-CLAAANK

THE COFFRET HEART...
IT BUSTED OPEN...

WHAT'RE YOU STARING AT...?
OH, WHATEVER THAT IS ON THE GROUND FELL OUT OF YOUR THING JUST NOW.

"I BROUGHTCHA A GIFT... TO HELP YA FEEL BETTER..."
SHHP

UH!
I WONDER IF THERE'S SOMETHIN' INSIDE.
HOLD OFF ON THAT...

Dear Se-chan,
I'll always love you.
Kokoro
...AND HE RAISED HIS HANDS MIDAIR!
THERE'S A TRIPLE LUTZ, A TRIPLE TOE LOOP...
THAT'S A VERY DIFFICULT JUMP!

SO FAR, HE HASN'T MADE ANY MAJOR ERRORS.
IT LOOKS LIKE KIJINAMI IS GOING ALL OUT TO TAKE FIRST PLACE THIS TIME!
I'LL ALWAYS...
...LOVE YOU.
OH, GOD...
I CAN'T HOLD IT IN ANY-MORE...

HEY, MEATBALL HEAD.

ARE YOU OKAY?

I...

I *DO* LOVE KOKORO-KUN.

BUT...

...PLEASE DON'T TELL ANYONE.

YOU'RE RIGHT, MORIYAMA-SAN. I ALWAYS WANNA BE WITH KOKOPPE...

AND THAT'S WHY WE GOTTA KEEP THINGS JUST HOW THEY ARE NOW...

CHIK

LET'S SEE...
CLACK
NOTHING'S BROKEN, SO IT SHOULD BE FINE.

HERE, JUST LIKE IT WAS.

AND DON'T WORRY.
YOUR FEELINGS ARE SAFE IN MY AMPLE BOSOM.

MORI-YAMA-SAN...
OKAY, LET'S GO. OUR GUY SHOULD BE COMING BACK ANY MINUTE NOW.

THAT WAS A RISKY MOVE YOU PULLED THERE.

IF THE JUDGES DOWNGRADE YOUR QUAD LUTZ, IT WON'T EVEN BE WORTH HALF AS MUCH AS A 4T.

Smiling for the camera.

IT WAS FOUR ROTATIONS. IT'LL BE FINE.

OHHH, AND IT'S A HIGH ONE!

AND KIJINAMI'S SCORE IS IN...

HE EARNED 160.37 POINTS IN THE FREE SKATE, MAKING HIS TOTAL SCORE 242.08!

WOW!

KOKORO
KOKORO
Kijinami Kokoro
KOKORO KIJINAMI HAS TAKEN FIRST PLACE!

IT'S THE BIRTH OF A NEW CHAMPION!
EEEEKKKK!!!
WE'RE GOING TO BE BUSY FROM NOW ON!
THERE'S A BIG DIFFERENCE BETWEEN GOING TO WORLDS AS CHAMPION VERSUS GOING AS SECOND-BEST.
FIRST, WE'LL HAVE TO ORGANIZE OUR INTERVIEW SCHEDULE!

MORIYAMA-SAN WAS RIGHT.
AFTER THAT, THE REST OF THE EVENT WAS A BLUR OF ONE THING AFTER ANOTHER.

I BARELY HAD THE CHANCE TO SAY A WORD TO KOKOPPE, AND THEN WE WERE BACK IN TOKYO.

BUT THAT STILL DOESN'T GIVE YOU THE RIGHT TO TAKE ADVANTAGE OF MY EMPLOYEE.
Kodan Publishing

HMM...

Nacinamin A

Dec. 25th Yon Sports

Japan Figure Skati

Kijinami Tak

A new champion

IF UPPER MANAGEMENT FOUND OUT ABOUT WHAT IGARI'S UP TO...
WELL, THEY PROBABLY WOULDN'T FIRE HER.

BUT STILL... WHAT IF WORSE COMES TO WORSE? WHAT IF I HAVE TO TELL HER SHE'S BEING LET GO...?
THEN AGAIN, MAYBE I COULD HIRE HER MYSELF...
WOULD YOU LIKE DINNER, BOSS? OR SHALL I PREPARE YOUR BATH?

FWISH FWISH FWISH FWISH
WHAT AM I THINKING? I CAN'T JUST HIRE HER TO BE MY HOUSEWIFE!
EXCUSE ME, SAWADA-KUN?

BWAH?! DIRECTOR SUGITA-SAN?!
IS SOME-THING THE MATTER?
I'M LOOKING FOR A LADY FROM YOUR DEPARTMENT. IGARI-KUN?

THEY FOUND OUT ALREADY?!
D-DID SHE DO SOME-THING...?
BADUUUMP

WELL, HERE'S THE THING.
WE'RE BOOSTING *SASSO'S* CIRCULATION BY 10,000 COPIES THIS SPRING.

WHAT ...?

AND IN RETURN...

...THERE'S SOMETHING WE'D LIKE HER TO WORK ON.

Gaaah!

I'm laaate!

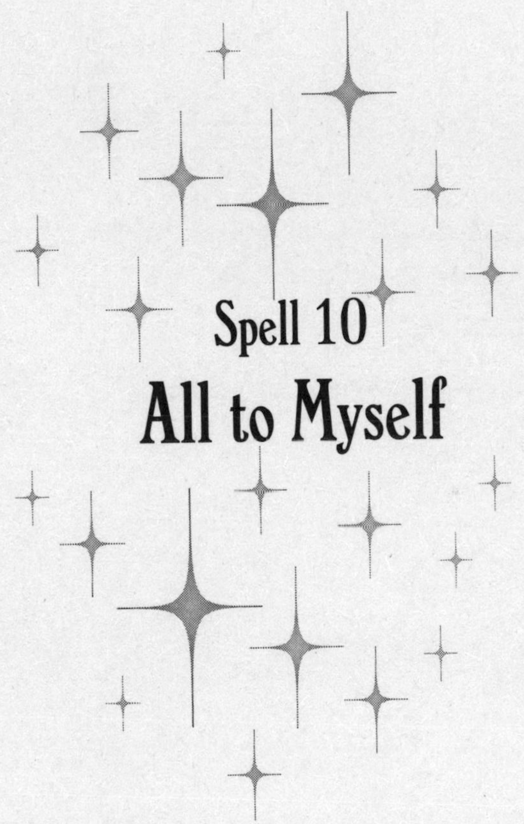

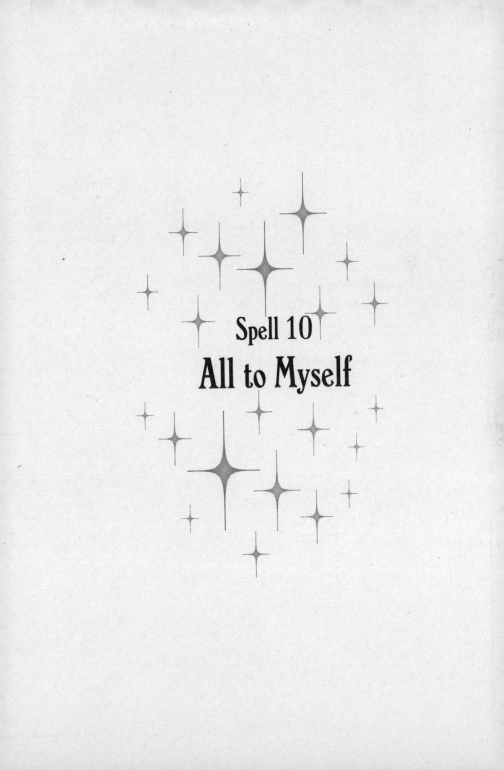

Spell 10
All to Myself

THERE'S THIS THING I STILL THINK ABOUT SOMETIMES.

AFTER I STARTED COLLEGE, A GUY TOLD ME HE LIKED ME FOR THE FIRST TIME EVER.

I WAS OVERJOYED. SO, I CHANGED MY HAIRSTYLE AND THE WAY I DRESSED TO TRY TO BETTER MATCH HIS TASTE.

"HEY, MIND IF I'M KIND OF BLUNT?"

"THAT LOOK REALLY DOESN'T SUIT YOU."

MUCH MORE THAN THE ACTUAL REASON WE BROKE UP...

FOR SOME REASON, THAT'S WHAT STILL HURTS.

OH. MY. GOD!!
KIJINAMI-KUN IS JUST TOO COOL!
Zaroff
COFFEE

www.house-of-zaroff.com

DID YOU HEAR? HE DID A QUAD LUXE!

HUH? WHAT'S THAT, MANAGER?

NATIONALS ARE OVER NOW...

OH, RIGHT. I MEAN A LUTZ.

...AND KOKOPPE IS THE NEW CHAMPION. HE'S ALWAYS HAD A LOT OF FEMALE FANS.

AND ACCORDING TO MORIYAMA-SAN, THIS WIN SENT HIS "MARKET VALUE" SKY-ROCKETING.

Note: a male fan.

CAN YOU BELIEVE THE MANAGER WAS SO EXCITED, HE MADE A NEW MENU ITEM FOR THE OCCASION?

IT'S A FOUR-CHEESE SANDWICH CALLED THE SPECIAL QUAD. ♡

Doesn't it look good?

NEW!

ANYWAY, I'M SURPRISED YOU'RE DRINKING COFFEE THIS MORNING, IGARI-CHAN!

You usually have plum hojicha!

OH...YEAH. WELL, I HAVE AN IMPORTANT MEETING COMING UP.

STILL...

...I NEVER THOUGHT I WAS GOING TO END UP IN A POSITION WHERE I HAD TO "MARKET" HIM.

...SO, OUR EDITORIAL DEPARTMENT WILL PICK A TITLE OUT OF THESE THREE OPTIONS.

IF POSSIBLE, IT WOULD BE HELPFUL TO DO A PHOTO SHOOT FOR THE FIRST ISSUE'S COVER AND MARKETING MATERIALS.

YOU'RE TOO KIND.

BUT BE AWARE THAT WE'LL HAVE SCHEDULING PRIORITY.

ANOTHER MAJOR COMPETITION IS COMING UP IN FEBRUARY, AFTER ALL.

OF COURSE.

I APPRECIATE HOW EASY YOU ARE TO NEGOTIATE WITH.

I SUPPOSE I SHOULD EXPECT NOTHING LESS FROM THE MUCH PRAISED EDITOR-IN-CHIEF OF *SASSO*.

HAHA... YOU FLATTER ME.

She certainly asserts herself...

DIRECTOR SUGITA ASSIGNED US THIS NEW PROJECT OUT OF NOWHERE...

SASSO IS GOING TO START DOING A FEATURE ON KOKOPPE'S HEALTH AND FITNESS REGIMEN IN EVERY ISSUE.

IGARI, DO YOU HAVE THOSE CHARACTER DESIGNS WE REQUESTED FROM OGATA-SAN?

YES, SIR. SHE DIDN'T HAVE MUCH TIME THOUGH, SO THEY'RE VERY ROUGH.

UHH, THIS IS... ME.

AND...

AND HERE'S KIJINAMI.

I THINK SHE MADE YOUR CHARACTER TOO PRETTY.
WOMEN ARE THE TARGET AUDIENCE HERE, SO SOMETHING CUTESIER WOULD BE BEST.
WOULD YOU ASK HER TO REVISE THIS? IT CAN WAIT UNTIL AFTER NEW YEAR'S.
Y-YES, SIR.
...I'M GOING TO HAVE TO WRITE FOR IT AS HIS "PERSONAL TRAINER."

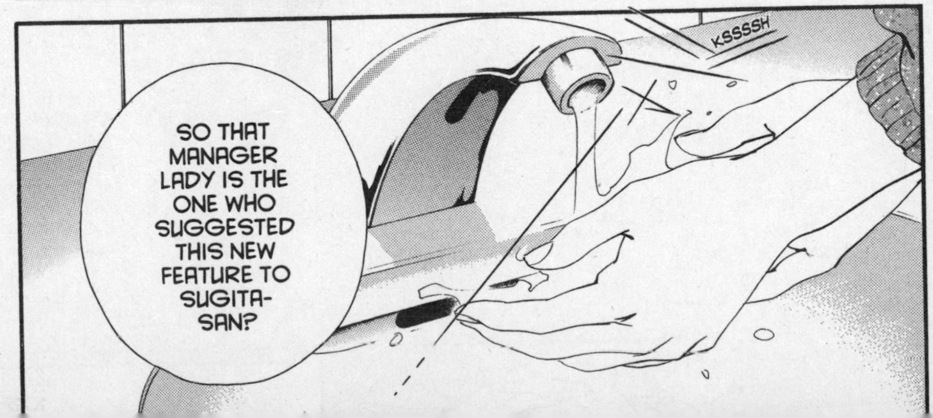

KSSSSH
SO THAT MANAGER LADY IS THE ONE WHO SUGGESTED THIS NEW FEATURE TO SUGITA-SAN?

HE'S MY LITTLE PIGGY.
Y-YEAH, BEATS ME...
I'LL JUST ASSUME THAT WAS A JOKE...

I WONDER HOW THEY KNOW EACH OTHER.
SAWADA-SAN SAYS IT'S SOME KIND OF PERSONAL CONNECTION, BUT I DON'T KNOW.

ANYWAY, I WAS PRETTY SURPRISED TO FIND OUT YOU AND KOKORO KIJINAMI WERE CHILDHOOD FRIENDS, IGA-CHAN.
BUT ARE YOU *SURE* YOU CAN HANDLE BEING A TOP ATHLETE'S PERSONAL TRAINER? I KNOW IT'S JUST A FRONT, BUT STILL...
WELL...

HIS ORIGINAL TRAINER IS GOING TO KEEP TAKING CARE OF THE ACTUAL TRAINING.
AND I DID STUDY EXERCISE PHYSIOLOGY IN COLLEGE...
BUT MY ONLY CERTIFICA-TION IS A NUTRITIONIST'S LICENSE.

SO, I THOUGHT I'D LOOK INTO GETTING CERTIFIED AS A REGISTERED DIETITIAN OR ATHLETIC TRAINER BEFORE THE OLYMPICS.
WH-OA!
THE OLYMPICS ARE ONLY TWO YEARS AWAY!

ALTHOUGH, MAYBE IT'S DOABLE IF YOU HAVE OUR BOSS'S PERMISSION...
BUT DON'T PUSH YOURSELF TOO HARD, IGA-CHAN! YOU HAVE YOUR HEALTH TO CONSIDER.

I KNOW. DON'T WORRY.
I KNOW I'VE GOT MY WORK CUT OUT FOR ME, AND I'M ALREADY FEELING THE PRESSURE...

BUT STILL...
"I DO LOVE KOKORO-KUN."
EVER SINCE I SAID THAT...
12
Reference Document A
Profile on Kokoro Kijinami
ents
(Provisional)

...I'VE STARTED FEELING LIKE I'M FLOATING ON CLOUD NINE EVERY TIME I THINK ABOUT KOKOPPE.

I KNOW THIS WILL BE AN ORDEAL, BUT I CAN'T HELP FEELING EXCITED, LIKE I'M BEING REWARDED.

HEY, MAMA! CHITOSE'S HERE.
WAIT UP, YUUKI. COULDJA HELP ME WITH MY BAGS?

OOOH, TOKYO BANANAS.
Don't mind if I do.
WOULDJA LIKE SOME TEA?
GIMME A SEC. I'M GONNA PAY MY RESPECTS TO GRAMMY.

DIIIIING

...OH, GRAMMY.
THANK YOU FOR ALWAYS WATCHIN' OVER ME.
IT'S HELPED ME STAY POSITIVE.

KO-KOPPE'S DOIN' GOOD, TOO.
HE WON THE BIGGEST COMPETITION IN JAPAN, AND NOW HE'S RIGHT FAMOUS.

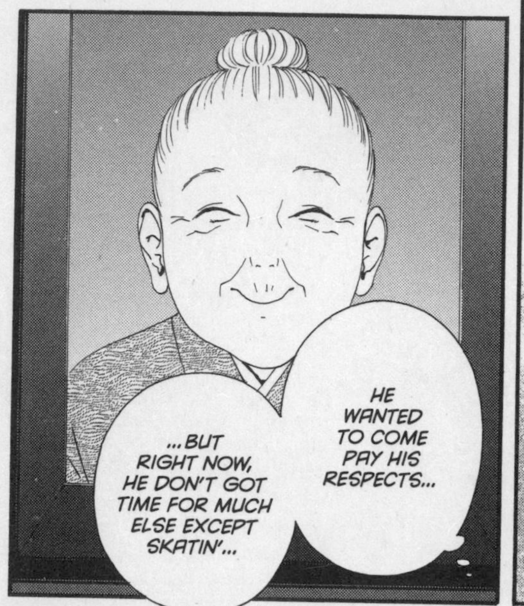
HE WANTED TO COME PAY HIS RESPECTS...
...BUT RIGHT NOW, HE DON'T GOT TIME FOR MUCH ELSE EXCEPT SKATIN'...

YA MEAN KOKORO-KUN CAN'T EVEN GO VISIT HIS FAMILY?
WELL,
HE SAID THE TRAVEL WOULD BE TOO MUCH FOR HIM. AFTER ALL, NEW YEAR'S IS THE ONLY DAY HE GETS OFF, AND THAT'S IF HE'S LUCKY.

BEING THE NATIONAL FIGURE SKATING CHAMPION'S A ROUGH JOB, HUH?
THAT'S RIGHT.
EVEN *I* HAVEN'T SEEN HIM SINCE WE WERE IN OSAKA.

THANKS TO THAT...
...I'VE BEEN ABLE TO ACT LIKE I DIDN'T SEE THAT NOTE...
YOU SHOULD GET HIS AUTOGRAPH FOR ME, NEE-CHAN.

AND SO, CAME THE NEW YEAR...
WHAT ?!
Kodan Publishing
kae
N-
NUDES ?!

HE *IS* AN ATHLETE, SO WE SHOULD USE PHOTOS THAT SHOW OFF THE MUSCULAR PHYSIQUE HE'S WORKED SO HARD FOR!
DON'T YOU THINK IT'S A GOOD IDEA, BOSS?

N-
NO NO NO!
F-FIGURE SKATERS HAVE TO KEEP THEIR REPUTATION CLASSY!
WE CAN'T!
AWW.

ACTUALLY, I THINK IT'S WORTH LOOKING INTO.
I DON'T IMAGINE THERE'D BE A PROBLEM AS LONG AS WE GO THROUGH HIS MANAGER. IT'S NOT LIKE HE'S A GIRL.
RIGHT? I WAS THINKING THE SAME THING!

OH, GOD... IF MORIYAMA-SAN GAVE THE ORDER, I BET KOKOPPE WOULD JUST GO ALONG WITH IT.
STRIP.
YES, MA'AM.
IF I DON'T PUT A STOP TO THIS, THE WHOLE COUNTRY COULD SEE HIM BUCK NAKED...

NO!
KOKOP-KOKORO-KUN HAS A MARK ON HIS SIDE THAT NO ONE CAN SEE!

YOU...

...AND KOKORO KIJINAMI MUST BE PRETTY CLOSE FOR YOU TO HAVE SEEN THIS MARK OF HIS.

...HUH?
BUUUH?

OH!
N—
NO! W-W-WE JUST GO WAY BACK, Y'KNOW!
WE WERE KIDS! I SAW IT WHEN WE WERE LITTLE!
ボン
BLUSH

I-I BETTER HEAD TO THE STUDIO!
EXCUSE ME!
ひゅん
ZOOOOM

WHAT'S HER DEAL?
DOES SHE THINK I'M GOING TO BELIEVE HER WHEN SHE CAN'T EVEN DENY IT WITHOUT HER FACE TURNING BRIGHT RED?
GRRR.

AFTER THAT, "KOKORO-KUN'S MARK" BECAME A TRENDING TOPIC IN THE OFFICE.
It has to be a bleeep.
Maybe he talks to it, like a tulpa or something.

KIJINAMI-SAN IS HERE!
GET READY, EVERYONE.
BA-DUMP
...OH, HEY.
PLEASE, LET ME TAKE CARE OF YOUR THINGS.
YOU CAN LEAVE YOUR SHOES ON.

OKAY, LET ME BREAK THINGS DOWN FOR YOU. WE'LL START WITH THE COVER PHOTOS...
BE STILL MY BEATING HEART...
BADUMP
BADUMP
BADUMP
IT-IT'S BEEN A WHILE, HASN'T IT?
SEEMS LIKE YOU'RE DOIN' GOOD.
YEAH... YOU, TOO, SE-CHAN.
FLASH

FLASH
FLASH
NICE, I LIKE IT!
NOW, LOOK OVER HERE.
FLASH
ALL RIGHT, GOT IT.

BUT I CAN FEEL HIS EYES WHEN HE LOOKS AT ME LIKE THAT.

IT MAKES IT HARD TO EVEN BREATHE...

HELLO?
OH, YES. ...HUH?
OSAKA...? TOMORROW?!

I TOLD YOU KIJINAMI WOULD BE APPEARING IN A JEWELRY COMMERCIAL, DIDN'T I?
WELL, THE COMPANY'S GOING TO SHOW IT AT THEIR NEWEST BOUTIQUE'S GRAND OPENING TOMORROW.
I'VE ARRANGED TO HAVE IT COVERED BY A FEW DIFFERENT MEDIA OUTLETS, SO YOU SHOULD COME, TOO.

WH-WHAT FOR?
WHAT DO YOU MEAN, WHAT FOR?!
HOW ELSE ARE WE SUPPOSED TO SELL OUR STORY TO THE PUBLIC?!
B-BUT...

THIS IS TOO SUDDEN. I DON'T HAVE TIME TO—
I'VE ALREADY MADE ALL THE ARRANGEMENTS.
I'LL SEND SASSO THE INVOICE LATER.
I'LL EMAIL YOU THE DETAILS.
REGISTERED DIETITIAN CERTIFICATION MADE EASY
CLICK

ALL FOR A COM-
MERCIAL, HUH...?
JUST WINNING COMPETITIONS WAS ALREADY HARD ENOUGH...
SIIIGH...

KOKOPPE HAS ALWAYS BEEN A SOFTY.
CAN HE MAKE IT IN SUCH A CUTTHROAT WORLD?
NOW, KOKOPPE, YA GOTTA LEARN TO EAT YOUR BOILED WHITEBAIT.
NUH-UH, THEY'RE LOOKIN' AT ME...
COME NOW! THEY AIN'T LOOKIN' AT YA!

IF BEIN' THERE WITH HIM LETS ME PROTECT HIM, EVEN JUST A LITTLE...
...THEN I KNOW WHAT I GOTTA DO!

THE SHOP WHERE THE PARTY'S BEING HELD IS RIGHT IN FRONT OF OUR HOTEL, SO WE CAN GET READY HERE.

Y-YOU WANT ME TO WEAR... *THAT?*
YEAH.

JUST LIKE I THOUGHT, YOU SHOWED UP DRESSED LIKE A PEASANT.
DID YOU EVEN CONSIDER THE OCCASION? COME ON NOW. TAKE IT OFF!
ACK, HEY!
WAIT!

M-MY UNDER-WEAR, TOO?!
DUH. I CAN'T BELIEVE YOU CAME WEARING A SPORTS BRA.
WAS I RIGHT THAT YOU'RE A 30B? ...OH WOW, NOT BAD, IF YOU GIVE THEM A LITTLE LIFT AND PRESS THEM TOGETHER.
SQUEEZE ぎゅう
SQUEEZE ぎゅう
WAAAGH, QUIT GRABBIN' MY BOOBS!

EEEEEEEEEKK!!
HAIR WAX
...PHEW.

LOOK.

PRETTY AMAZING, HUH?

I CAN BARELY STAND IN THESE HEELS...

AND I'M SHOWING SO MUCH LEG AND CLEAVAGE... IT'S TOO EMBARRASSING...

NO!

IT'S ONLY EMBARRASSING BECAUSE YOU'RE *ACTING* EMBARRASSED!

TO SHOW OFF RIGHT, YOU'VE GOT TO BE BOLD!

KA-BAM

BEHOLD THE MAJESTY OF MY TWIN ROCKETS!

OH, YOU POOR THING. DON'T YOU HAVE ANY DESIRE TO TAKE THIS CHANCE TO BAG KIJINAMI?
You sound like you're from the sixties...
B-BAG...?
TH-THERE'S NO WAY THAT COULD HAPPEN...

I MEAN... GETTING ALL DRESSED UP LIKE THIS...
...JUST DOESN'T SUIT ME.

"HEY, MIND IF I'M KIND OF BLUNT?"
"THAT LOOK REALLY DOESN'T SUIT YOU."

WHAT?
IS THAT SOMETHING A MAN SAID TO YOU?
Fig. 1: heart
BA-DONK

SO YOU OVERDID YOUR MAKEUP OR SOME-THING, AND HE CRITICIZED YOU FOR IT. RIGHT?
WELL, MEMORIES OF A GUY LIKE THAT ARE WORTH ABOUT AS MUCH AS YESTERDAY'S GARBAGE.

H-HOW DID YOU...?
GAH!!
LET ME GUESS.
YOU WENT TO COLLEGE, STARTED LIVING ON YOUR OWN, FOUND A BOY-FRIEND, AND THOUGHT YOU'D BECOME A NEW WOMAN.

LISTEN, MEATBALL HEAD. YOU LOOK AMAZING RIGHT NOW.
HAVE SOME CONFIDENCE. GO GET YOUR MAN.

I'VE GOT TO WAIT FOR SOMEONE AT THE FRONT, SO YOU GO ON AHEAD.
KIJINAMI SHOULD ALREADY BE HERE.
A-ALL RIGHT...

LET'S SEE...

GLANCE GLANCE

WHERE'S KO-KOPPE...?

LOOK, IT'S KO-KORO-KUN!

SERI-OUSLY?! WHERE?!

HE'S OVER THERE WITH LIZA SHIBATA.

WHO'S THAT AGAIN?

A MODEL. SHE'S PRETTY POPULAR LATELY. I HEAR THE TWO OF THEM ARE GOING TO BE IN A COMMERCIAL TOGETHER.

HMM, THEY *DO* SEEM LIKE THEY SUIT EACH OTHER...

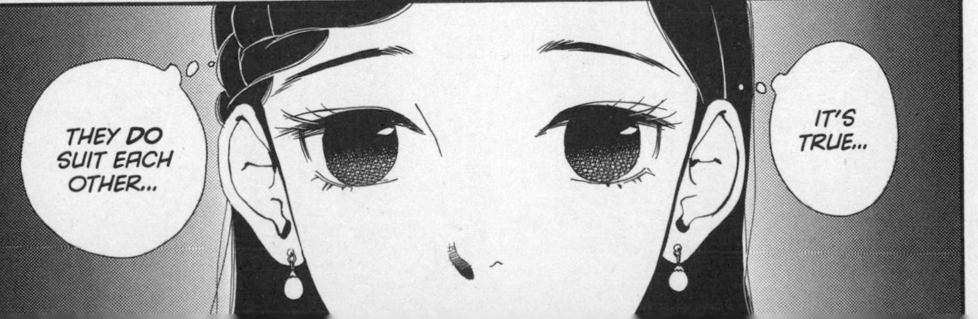

HER STYLE, HER FACE, EVERYTHING ABOUT HER IS A BETTER MATCH FOR KOKOPPE.
SHE'S BEAU-TIFUL...

AND HERE I AM...

SE-CHAN...?
WHAT ARE YOU DOING DRESSED LIKE THAT?
OH...

"LISTEN, MEATBALL HEAD. YOU LOOK AMAZING RIGHT NOW."
RIGHT. I HAVE TO BE CONFIDENT.
M... MORIYAMA-SAN PICKED OUT THIS OUTFIT FOR ME...

FWISH
HUH?!

WAIT...
KOKOPPE, WHAT'S—
YA GOTTA CHANGE CLOTHES.
WHA...?

SE-CHAN...
THAT LOOK JUST DON'T SUIT YOU!

HEY, MIND IF I'M KIND OF BLUNT?
THAT LOOK...
...DOESN'T SUIT YOU.

...THAT.
SE-CHAN...?
ボコッ
BONK!!
YA DON'T GOTTA SAY IT!
I *KNOW* THAT ALREADY!

SE-
CHAN!

ARE YOU OKAY, KIJINAMI-KUN?
Your nose is bleeding!
CLASP
がしっ
OH, UH, YEAH—
WHAT'S HER PROB-LEM?!

I'M DONE.

I JUST WANT TO SHRIVEL UP AND DISAPPEAR.

AAHH!

SHWUP

WHAT THE HELL?
IS THAT *YOU*, IGARI?

B-BOSS.
IS THE PARTY OVER ALREADY? I THOUGHT I WAS GOING TO JUST BARELY MAKE IT.
OH, NO...

DAMN, THOUGH. YOU CERTAINLY GOT ALL DRESSED UP FOR THE OCCASION.
YOU LOOK GOOD.

SQUEEE

WOULD YOU ESCORT ME TO MY HOTEL ROOM?

UH, SURE.
ALL RIGHT.

KIJI-NAMI-KUN.
YOU GO BACK TO THE PARTY. YOU HAVE THAT PRESS CONFERENCE OF YOURS, AFTER ALL.

...THANK YOU.
NO PROBLEM.
I'M GOING TO HEAD BACK TO THE PARTY NOW.

BY THE WAY...
IS THERE ANYTHING YOU'D LIKE ME TO TELL KOKORO KIJINAMI?

...NOT REALLY...
NO...

REALLY?
WELL THEN, I'M OFF.

IT'S ALMOST TIME, LIZA. LET ME FIX YOUR MAKEUP.
OKAY.

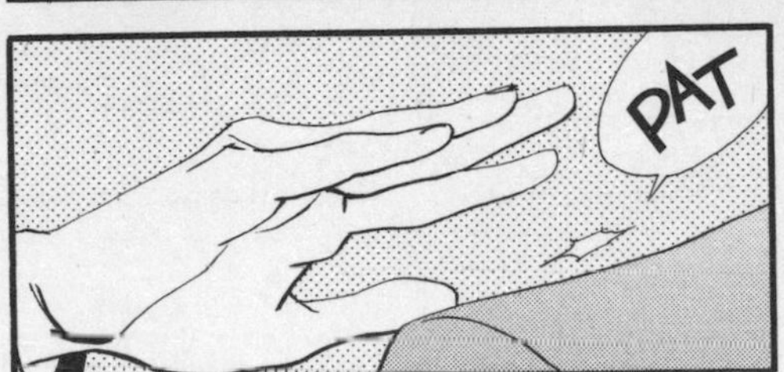

PAT

SA-WADA-SAN...?
LOOKS LIKE I'M JUST IN TIME.

IGARI WANTED ME TO LET YOU KNOW.
SHE SAID, "GOOD LUCK AT YOUR PRESS CONFERENCE."

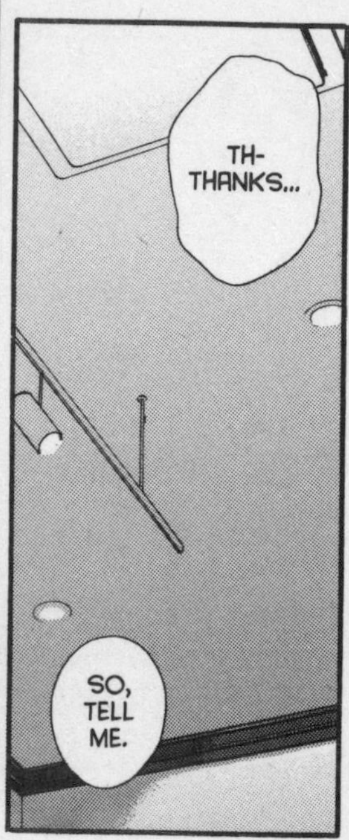
TH- THANKS...
SO, TELL ME.

WHAT DID YOU SAY TO HER?

I MEAN... JUST... SHE WASN'T DRESSED ANYTHING LIKE HER USUAL SELF...
SO, I SAID IT DIDN'T SUIT HER...
REALLY? I THOUGHT SHE LOOKED QUITE NICE.

NO, I-I THOUGHT SHE WAS PRETTY... JUST...
I MEAN... WITH ALL THESE PEOPLE HERE, AND...
UHH...
You know, this and that.
She's just so dang adorable.

BABY'S NOT USED TO FEELING JEALOUS, HUH? JUST LIKE I THOUGHT.
IF THERE'S ANYTHING YOU WANT TO TELL HER, I CAN PASS IT ALONG.

...

PLEASE TELL HER...
"I'LL DO MY BEST AT THE PRESS CONFERENCE."

YOU GOD DAMN
MIDDLE SCHOOLER.

DEE DEE DEEEEE-

Kokoppe

KOKOPPE SENT ME A TEXT...

BLUSH

LTE
74%
From: ☆Kokoppe
To: Se-chan
About your outfit today
Would you wear it next time we're alone together?
Kokoro

A-AM I DOIN' IT RIGHT...?
SAWADA COACHED HIM.

I'LL HAVE TO THANK SAWADA-SAN.

"HOW ABOUT WHEN WE'RE DONE WITH THIS SEASON'S COMPETITIONS?"... THERE.
I GET THE FEELING HE'S HELPED KOKOPPE AND ME GET A LITTLE CLOSER...

BRRRRRRING
BUT A FEW DAYS LATER...
dan Publishing

SASSO EDITORIAL DEPARTMENT.
UH-HUH, YES.
YES...

THE NEWS CAME SO FAST.

SASSO HAD JUST ORGANIZED OUR SUPPORT TEAM FOR KOKOPPE.

AND NOW, WE WERE ALL GOING TO BE PUT TO THE TEST.

DEPENDING ON WHAT THEY SAY, HE MAY HAVE TO BOW OUT OF THE FOUR CONTINENTS CHAMPIONSHIPS.

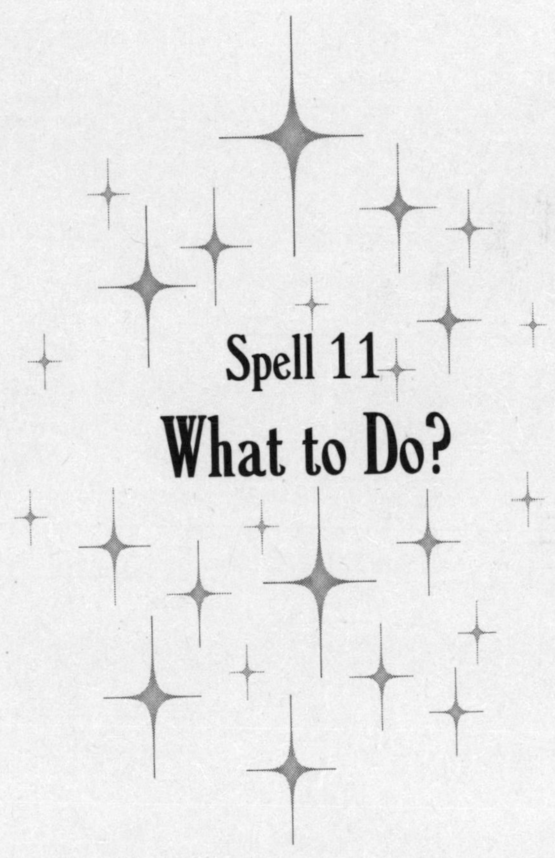

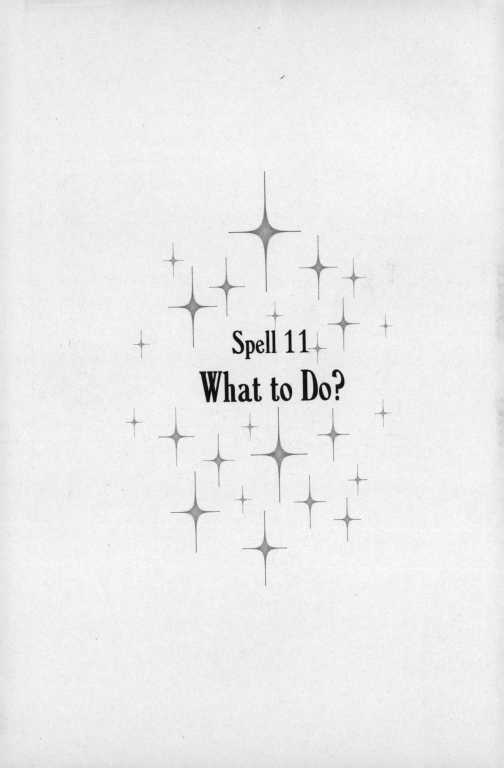

Spell 11
What to Do?

EVERY LINE AND CURVE SPARKLES WITH MAGIC...

A SILVER GLOW BEFITTING A GODDESS...

AND SO BEGINS YOUR PERSONAL PLATINUM STORY...

HEY!

ANYWAY, I GUESS THIS'LL BE HIS ONE LONELY COMMERCIAL PLAYING DURING THE FOUR CONTINENTS CHAMPIONSHIPS...
HIS HEALTH AND PERFORMANCE CAN AFFECT SO MANY DIFFERENT THINGS.
SEEMS EXHAUSTING.
I MEAN, YEAH, BUT STILL...

WHY'D YOU TURN OFF KOKORO-KUN'S COMMERCIAL?
ALL THAT HAPPENS NEXT IS LIZA SHIBATA SHOWS UP TO LOOK PRETTY.
SORRY, BUT THAT'S WHERE MY HOME RECORDING ENDS, TOO.

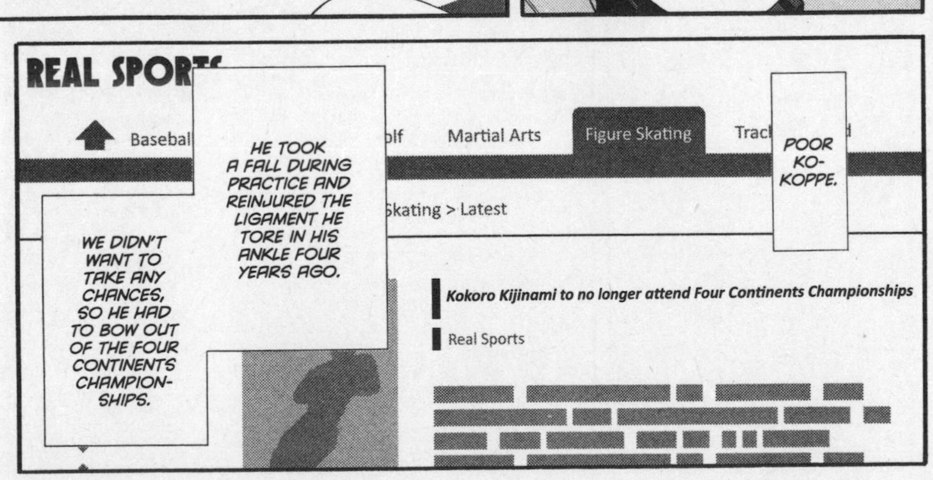

REAL SPORTS
Basebal
olf
Martial Arts
Figure Skating
Track
Skating > Latest
Kokoro Kijinami to no longer attend Four Continents Championships
Real Sports
POOR KO-KOPPE.
HE TOOK A FALL DURING PRACTICE AND REINJURED THE LIGAMENT HE TORE IN HIS ANKLE FOUR YEARS AGO.
WE DIDN'T WANT TO TAKE ANY CHANCES, SO HE HAD TO BOW OUT OF THE FOUR CONTINENTS CHAMPIONSHIPS.

MEANWHILE, WITH 10,000 COPIES ADDED TO OUR CIRCULATION, SASSO HAD BIG PLANS FOR A REPORT ON THE FOUR CONTINENTS FOR OUR FIRST KOKOPPE ISSUE. BUT NOW...

...I WANT YOU TO LOOK AT THIS SITUATION AS AN OPPORTUNITY.

STARTING FROM LESS-THAN-IDEAL CIRCUMSTANCES MAY NOT BE FUN, BUT WE CAN STILL BUILD ENGAGEMENT.

AIM TO SUPPORT KIJINAMI THROUGH HIS RECOVERY AND ENABLE HIM TO DO WELL AT THE WORLD CHAMPIONSHIPS.

FOR EXAMPLE, TO GET CERTIFIED AS A REGISTERED DIETITIAN, I WOULD NEED TO WORK SIX-HOUR DAYS AS A NUTRITIONIST AT LEAST FOUR TIMES A WEEK FOR A YEAR.
SO, TO MAKE THAT WORK, I'D SPLIT MY TIME HERE INTO TWO SHIFTS: MORNING AND NIGHT.

IT SAYS HERE YOU'D SPEND YOUR WEEKENDS SHADOWING KIJINAMI'S TRAINER, TOO.
WHEN WOULD YOU STUDY FOR THE EXAM?
SUNDAYS... AND WHEN-EVER I HAVE A SPARE MOMENT DURING MY COMMUTES OR MEAL BREAKS.

ALSO, THIS FITNESS PROGRAMMER CERTIFICATION SHOULD ACTUALLY BE PRETTY EASY FOR ME.
IGA-RI...
I ALREADY TOOK MOST OF THE CLASSES YOU NEED TO BE ELIGIBLE FOR THE EXAM WHEN I WAS IN COLLEGE.
IGARI.

STOP GETTING AHEAD OF YOURSELF.

DO YOU REALLY THINK YOU CAN HANDLE A SCHEDULE THIS TIGHT?
I KNOW YOU'RE GOOD AT YOUR JOB AND A HARD WORKER, BUT THAT DOESN'T CHANGE THE REALITY OF YOUR HEALTH CONDITION.
YOU'D JUST END UP PASSING OUT WITH A FEVER AGAIN.

I CAN UNDERSTAND YOUR DESIRE TO HELP KIJINAMI, BUT I WANT YOU TO RETHINK THIS.
WHAT'S IMPORTANT IS THE QUALITY OF YOUR WORK, NOT YOUR JOB TITLE.

KSSSSSH

...AND THE FOUR CONTINENTS FIGURE SKATING CHAMPIONSHIPS WILL BE HELD THIS WEEKEND IN COLORADO SPRINGS, UNITED STATES.
JAPAN WILL BE REPRESENTED IN ICE DANCING BY A TEAM OF THREE MEN AND THREE WOMEN, INCLUDING MAYO ASAMA.

HERE'S TAIGA AOKI, WHO ARRIVED AT THE SITE ON WEDNESDAY MORNING LOCAL TIME, ONLY TO JUMP STRAIGHT INTO AFTERNOON PRACTICE.
HE APPEARED TO BE DOING WELL, EVEN LANDING A QUAD-TRIPLE COMBO.

UN-FORTUNATELY, THE MEN'S CHAMPION, KOKORO KIJINAMI, SUSTAINED AN INJURY AND HAS HAD TO–
FWICK

SHH! NOT SO LOUD, HIKARU-KUN.
ANYWAY, IT'S POSSIBLE HIS INJURY FROM FOUR YEARS AGO STILL HASN'T FULLY HEALED.
A SPRAIN CAN LEAD TO CHRONIC PROBLEMS IF IT'S NOT TREATED PROPERLY RIGHT AWAY.

IF HE'D LISTENED TO ME OR HONDA-SAN WHEN WE TRIED TO TELL HIM NOT TO FIXATE SO HARD ON PRACTICING THAT ONE JUMP...
HE JUST NEVER LEARNS.

IS KOKORO'S INJURY REALLY THAT BAD?

WOW, PEGA-KUN, KOKOPPE'S SULKING IS PRETTY IMPRESSIVE.
WHAT CAN YOU DO, PEGA?
PEOPLE OVERTHINK THINGS WHEN THEY'RE STUCK IN BED, PEGA.
PLOOP
ひょこっ

OH YEAH! HE MUST BE WORRIED ABOUT WHAT SE-CHAN AND SAWADA GOT UP TO IN THAT HOTEL BACK IN OSAKA.
WOW, TALK ABOUT PARANOID, PEGA. HE SHOULD FOCUS ON SKATING.
I MEAN, REALISTICALLY, THERE'S NOTHING THEY COULD'VE DONE IN SUCH A SHORT TIME, PEGA.
It's jealousy!

OH, PEGA-KUN. YOU CAN'T EXPECT REALISM FROM A MAN WHO'S GONE 22 YEARS WITHOUT A GIRLFRIEND.
PFFT!
YEAH, I GUESS PORN GAMES ARE HIS ONLY REFERENCE, PEGA.

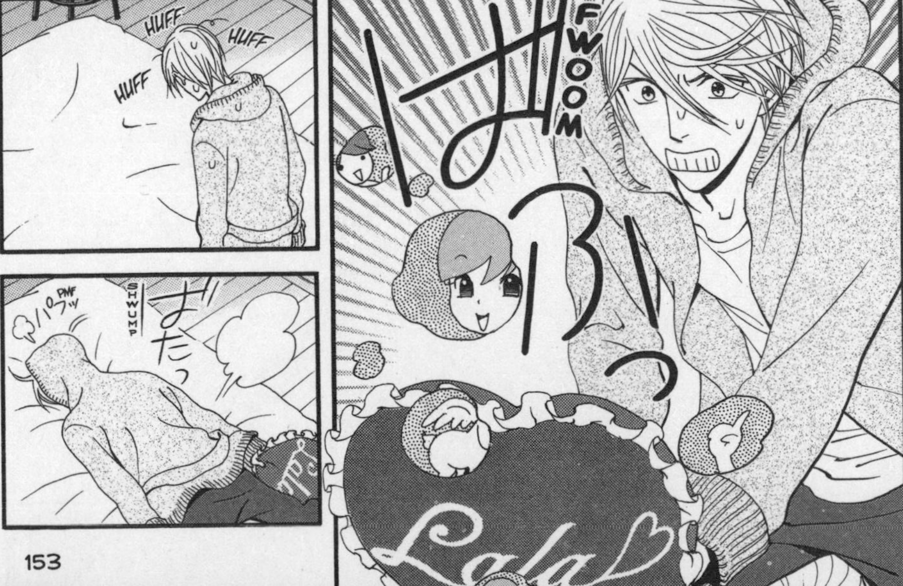
HUFF
HUFF
HUFF
FWOOM
SHWUMP
PMF
Lala

IF I STOP BEIN' ABLE TO LAND MY QUADS...

IS SE-CHAN GONNA...?

"THE QUALITY OF MY WORK"? *PLEASE!*

HE SHOULD KNOW I'M THE TYPE OF PERSON WHO TAPS, TAPS, TAPS ON A STONE BRIDGE UNTIL IT BREAKS BEFORE CROSSING IT!

YEAH, BUT IF IT *BREAKS,* YOU *CAN'T* CROSS IT..

I DIDN'T KNOW SHE GOT SO WILD WHEN SHE DRINKS.

SAWADA-SAN IS JUST WORRIED 'CAUSE HE CARES ABOUT YOU. HE CAN'T HELP IT.

WELL, THERE IS SUCH A THING AS *TOO MUCH* MEDDLING.

THAT'S RIGHT! HE'S MEDDLING TOO MUCH!

SORRY I MADE YOU WAIT AROUND FOR ME.

NO PROBLEM. I HAD SOME WORK TO FINISH UP ANYWAY.

I SUPPOSE WE'LL BE HITTING THE BAR WITH HOW LATE IT IS.

YANO-SAN FROM PR...?!

S-SERIOUSLY?! SHE AND SAWADA-SAN ARE A THING?!
I'M ACTUALLY PRETTY SURE MORE PEOPLE KNOW THAN DON'T.
IT'S BEEN THAT WAY SINCE BEFORE I STARTED WORKING HERE.
OF COURSE, EVERYONE'S CAREFUL NOT TO BRING IT UP. HEH.

I SEE... THEY'RE A GOOD MATCH, SINCE YANO-SAN'S SO PRETTY AND SEEMS GOOD AT HER JOB...
BUT WHY HAVEN'T THEY GOTTEN MARRIED?
IS IT BECAUSE OF WORK OR SOME-THING?

Order up! Fried gizzard's ready!
YOU REALLY *ARE* OUT OF THE LOOP, AREN'T YOU, IGA-CHAN?
I MEAN, YANO-SAN'S...

...MY HUSBAND'S AWAY ON BUSINESS. HE WON'T BE BACK TONIGHT.
CAN WE GO TO YOUR PLACE? IT'S BEEN A WHILE.

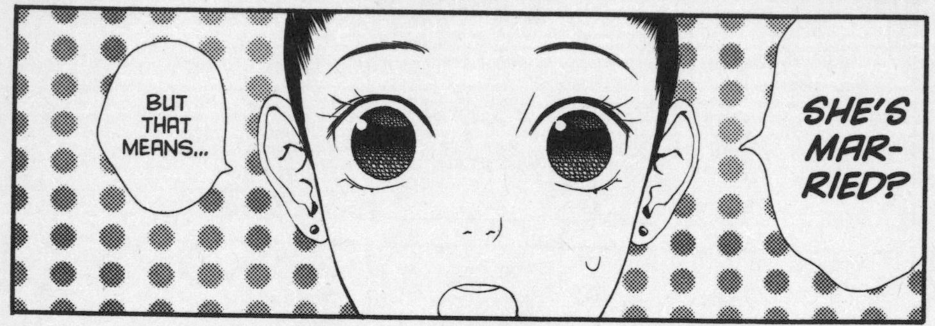

I DON'T KNOW THE DETAILS MYSELF.
RUMOR HAS IT THEY'VE BEEN DATING SINCE BEFORE YANO-SAN GOT MARRIED, THOUGH.
THEY TRIED BREAKING UP AT ONE POINT, BUT THINGS JUST KEEP HAPPENING.

NO STRINGS ATTACHED, HUH? SOUNDS VERY MATURE.
YEAH, I GUESS SO.
Not that I'd know.

HMM.
I GUESS MY BOSS'S RELATION-SHIPS ARE NONE OF MY BUSINESS, ANYWAY...
How about a mature relationship with me, senpai?
Not a chance.

BUT THERE'S SOMETHIN' ABOUT THIS...
...THAT JUST DON'T SIT RIGHT...

AFTER ALL, IF YOU START SCRAMBLING TO GET ALL KINDS OF QUALIFICATIONS NOW...
...YOU'LL BE SENDING EVERYONE THE MESSAGE THAT YOU'RE NOT QUALIFIED AT ALL.
E·H·S
GAH!

I AGREE WITH YOUR BOSS.

MOST PEOPLE WILL ASSUME YOU'RE QUALIFIED SOMEHOW, SINCE YOU WENT TO AN ATHLETICS-FOCUSED SCHOOL. SO, WHAT'S THE PROBLEM?
I'M GOING TO KEEP DOING THE ACTUAL TRAINING, JUST LIKE ALWAYS.
YEAH...

I GOT SICK AND HAD TO SPEND SOME TIME IN THE HOSPITAL WHEN I WAS IN COLLEGE.
AND I WAS ALREADY SO BUSY WITH MY NUTRITION AND EDUCATION CLASSES...
BUT I SHOULD'VE GONE FOR THAT FITNESS PROGRAMMER CERTIFICATION...
NOW, NOW.
I doubt I'll ever teach.
E

I KNOW THAT, BUT STILL...
I WANNA DO MORE... I WANNA MAKE MYSELF USEFUL TO KOKOPPE...

YOU'RE A LICENSED NUTRITIONIST, SO YOU MUST KNOW HOW TO COUNT CALORIES AND STUFF, RIGHT?
HERE'S AN IDEA. BEFORE HE RETIRED, TANAHASHI-KUN HAD A PERSONAL NUTRITIONIST WHO WOULD COOK FOOD FOR HIM TO SAVE AND EAT LATER.
DURING COMPETITIONS, THEY WOULD RENT A NEARBY APARTMENT FOR THE WEEK AND COOK THERE.
NOW, IF WE HIRED SOMEONE, I WOULD WANT A REGISTERED DIETITIAN TO DO THAT KIND OF THING.
BUT CONSIDERING YOU TWO ARE OLD FRIENDS, IT SHOULD BE FINE FOR YOU TO SUPPORT HIM THAT WAY.
Just don't charge us and we're good.
O-OH, I SEE.

COOKIN' FOR KOKOPPE, HUH?
THIS IS GREAT, SE-CHAN. ♡
IT'S LOW IN CALORIES, BUT FULL OF PROTEIN AND LOVE. ♡

W-WE'D BE LIKE NEWLY-WEDS OR SOME-THIN'...
ANYWAY, CHITOSE-CHAN.
HEH HEH! ♡

HUH ?!
WHAT I REALLY WANT YOUR HELP WITH IS THE PSYCHOLOGICAL SIDE OF THINGS.
WHAT DO YOU MAKE OF KOKORO-KUN LATELY?

OH...YEAH. WELL, I THINK GETTING HURT HAS DONE A NUMBER ON HIM.
HE'S BEEN KIND OF... STUCK IN HIS OWN HEAD...
OF COURSE, THAT'S NOT UNUSUAL FOR HIM, BUT STILL...

YEAH, I THINK YOU'RE RIGHT.
HE WAS PRACTICING THAT QUAD-RUPLE LUTZ WHEN HE GOT INJURED.
APPARENTLY, THE SAME THING HAPPENED WHEN HE HURT HIMSELF IN CANADA FOUR YEARS AGO.
AFTER THAT, HIS SLUMP LASTED ALL THE WAY UNTIL YOU CAME BACK INTO HIS LIFE...
...SO I'M A LITTLE WOR-RIED.

I AIN'T CUT OUT TO BE NUMBER ONE...

...
ANYWAY, KOKORO-KUN'S PRETTY LATE, HUH?
HE'S NOT ANSWERING HIS PHONE EITHER. WHAT COULD HE BE UP TO?

BY THE END OF THE NIGHT...

...KOKOPPE STILL HADN'T SHOWN UP FOR TRAINING.

...YOU WANNA GO CHECK UP ON HIM?

YOU WORRY TOO MUCH, DEAR.
BUT... HE MUST BE SO UPSET RIGHT NOW.
KOKORO'S FINE. MORIYAMA-SAN'S TAKIN' CARE OF THINGS.

OF COURSE HE'S UPSET.
HE'S CAUSIN' PROBLEMS FOR A LOT OF PEOPLE BY MISSIN' THAT COMPETITION.
HECK, IF THIS KINDA THING KEEPS UP, THE KIJINAMI GROUP'S STOCK PRICE COULD FALL.
DEAR... DON'T SAY THAT...
A BOY'S GOTTA FEEL SOME PRESSURE FROM TIME TO TIME TO BECOME A MAN.
BUT HE'S SO SENSITIVE...

THERE'S A STEP INTO A TRIPLE FLIP.
AND HE LANDS IT!
HIS STEPS ARE SO CLEAN AND PRECISE.
CLAIRE'S PERFOR-MANCES ARE ALWAYS FLAWLESS.

HE DIDN'T MAKE A SINGLE MISTAKE, BEATING HIS SEASON'S BEST.

IT'S GOING TO BE DIFFICULT FOR ANYONE TO MATCH SUCH A HIGH SCORE!

THE CURRENT LEADER IS CANADA'S LOUIS CLAIRE.

NOW, IT'S TIME FOR OUR FINAL SKATER TO TAKE TO THE ICE, AOKI OF JAPAN.

HAVE YOU TRIED CALLING HIM...? NOTHING?
ARE YOU SURE HE'S HOME?
THE LIGHTS ARE ON, AND I CAN HEAR THE TV, SO PROBABLY...
THEN JUST LET YOURSELF IN. THAT'S WHY I GAVE YOU A KEY.
B-BUT, I CAN'T JUST WALK INTO HIS APARTMENT...
NOT A PROBLEM, HUN. HE'S USED TO GETTING AMBUSHED BY ME.
HE SHOULD KNOW BY NOW TO SET THE CHAIN ON THE DOOR WHEN HE JACKS OFF.

OH...!

H-
HEY...

ARE YA HUNGRY?

I PICKED UP SOME HANDY LOOKIN' COOKIN' UTENSILS, TOO!
JUST GIMME A MINUTE.
Squash Mart

SO YEAH. IF YOU LIKE MY COOKIN', I'LL COME BY EVERY WEEK TO FIX YA A STOCK OF MEALS TO KEEP IN THE FREEZER.
I'LL BE MAKIN' SURE YOU GET ENOUGH CALORIES AND THE RIGHT NUTRITION, TOO. SOUNDS NICE, HUH?

UH-HUH...

HE WON'T EVEN LOOK AT ME...
GRRR.
WHATCHA UP TO?

DRAWIN'...

LADY LALA AGAIN?!
IS THAT WHAT YOU WERE DOIN' WHEN YOU WERE SUPPOSED TO BE GETTIN' PHYSICAL THERAPY, TOO?
Y'KNOW, TAKIGUCHI-SAN WAITED ALL NIGHT FOR YOU.

I CAN WORK OUT AT HOME.
IT'S JUST A SPRAIN...

JUST A SPRAIN...? WHO TOLD YOU THAT...?
A SPRAIN MEANS YOU'VE INJURED A LIGAMENT.
AND IF YOU DON'T START TAKIN' CARE OF IT, YOURS IS GONNA LEAD TO CHRONIC ISSUES...
HEY! ARE YOU EVEN LISTENIN' TO—
TMP
TMP
TMP
SHWIP
WAGH!

FWOMP
S... SORRY...

KO-KOPPE...?

WHAT'S THE MATTER? IS YOUR LEG—
QUIT TALKIN'.

JUST... STAY LIKE THAT.

SQUEEZE...

KO-
SE-
CHAN.
IF I QUIT
FIGURE
SKATING...
...WHAT'LL
YOU DO?

WH-WHAT DO YA MEAN?
WHAT IF I CAN NEVER JUMP AGAIN AND HAVE TO QUIT SKATIN'?
WHAT IF ALL YA WORK AT *SASSO* TURNS OUT TO BE FOR NOTHIN'?
YOU WOULDN'T HAVE A REASON TO HANG AROUND ANYMORE, SO—
DON'T BE STUPID!
CLENCH
ROLL

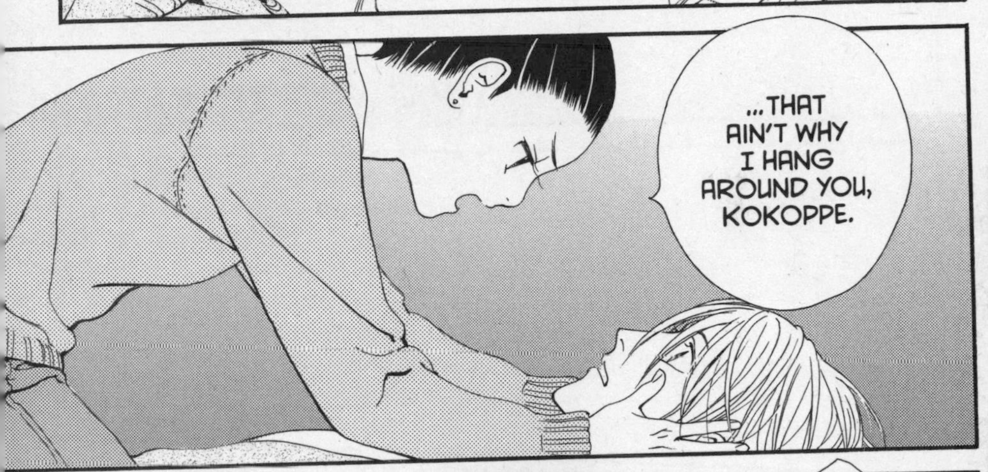

WHY ARE YOU TALKIN' ABOUT WHAT IF YOU CAN NEVER JUMP AGAIN?

DON'T YOU REALIZE WE'RE ALL WORKIN' TO MAKE SURE THAT ***DOESN'T*** HAPPEN?

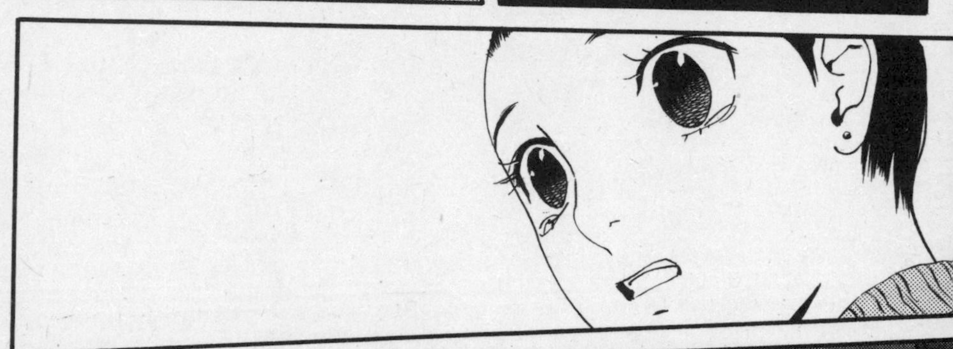

Layers
Layer 1
Layer 2
Layer 3
Layer 4
Layer 4 Copy
Layer 4 Copy 2
Layer 5
Background
Tools

...WHAT CAN I SAY?
YOU JUST LOOKED SO NICE THE OTHER DAY...

...WHAT AM I SUPPOSED TO DO?

WHAT WILL IT TAKE...
...FOR YOU TO GIVE SKATIN' YOUR ALL AGAIN, KOKOPPE?

...SAY I COMPETE IN THE WORLD CHAMPION-SHIPS...
IF I MAKE IT ONTO THE WINNERS' PODIUM...

...WILL YOU BE MY GIRL-FRIEND?
THIS TIME...
...I COULD FEEL KOKOPPE'S EYES FIXED ON MINE.

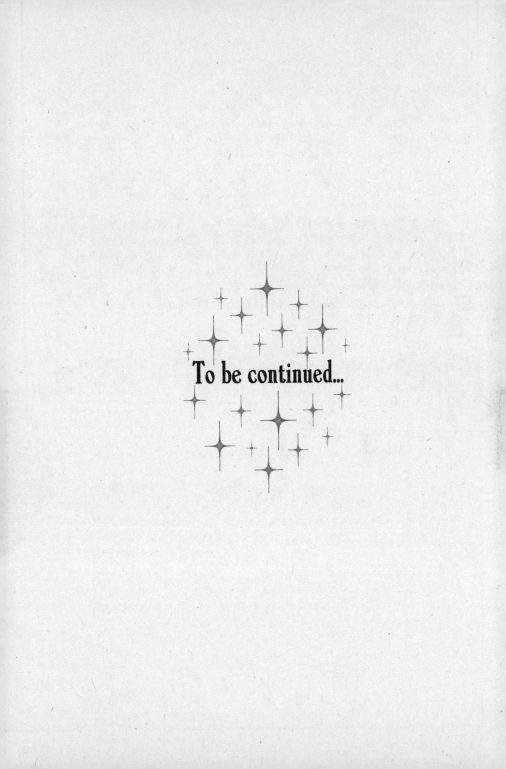

To be continued...

Translation Notes

Kiss and Never Cry, page 3

Kiss and Never Cry is another manga about figure skating—specifically, ice dancing—by Yayoi Ogawa, which Ogawa drew before *Knight of the Ice.* In it, Hikaru Yomota (Kokoro's assistant coach) is the ice dancing partner of Michiru, the main character. The series is eleven volumes long and was serialized in the josei manga magazine *Kiss* (the same magazine that serialized *Knight of the Ice)* between 2008 and 2011.

Mayo Asama, page 15

Similar to the fictional Densuke Tanahashi, the fictional Mayo Asama is based on world-renowned Japanese figure skater Mao Asada. Born in 1990, Asada is a four-time Grand Prix Final champion, a three-time Four Continents champion, a three-time World champion, and was a silver medalist in the 2010 Olympics, where she made history as the first female figure skater to land three triple Axel jumps in a single competition. In 2017, at the age of 27, Asada announced that she had retired from competitive figure skating.

Mami stan, page 22

Mami is the titular character from the 1980s anime series *Magical Angel Creamy Mami.* Given the anime's vintage year, it explains why Chitose follows up with jokingly asking Ogata how old she is.

Sendai, page 73

Sendai is the capital city of Miyagi Prefecture, and the largest city in Tohoku, a region of northern Japan.

Plum hojicha, page 106

Hojicha is a Japanese green tea, and plum *hojicha* is *hojicha* steeped with pickled plum. This is a low caffeinated tea, so it's surprising to find Chitose drinking coffee instead.

Tokyo Bananas, page 111

These aren't actually bananas! Despite what their name may imply, Tokyo Bananas are a cream-filled sponge cake shaped like a banana, and are the official souvenir sweet of Tokyo.

"He should know I'm the type of person who taps, taps, taps on a stone bridge until it breaks before crossing it!", page 155

Chitose is referring to the Japanese proverb *Ishibashi o tataite wataru,* or *Tap a stone bridge as you cross it.* The proverb warns that even stable bridges such as stone ones may have their cracks, so it's important to "tap" them—or to be cautious—to check for cracks and to stay on top of one's safety. Chitose is commenting on how diligent she is with her work, however, as her coworker points out, she has a tendency to overwork herself.

Aichi Prefecture, page 186

Aichi is an urban prefecture bordering the Pacific coast of the Chubu region of central Japan.

Garigari-kun popsicles, page 186

Garigari-kun is a popular brand of cheap popsicles widely available in Japanese convenience stores. The soda flavor is a classic.

Kiss, page 187

Kiss is a manga magazine targeting adult women published by Kodansha, and it's where *Knight of the Ice* was originally serialized.

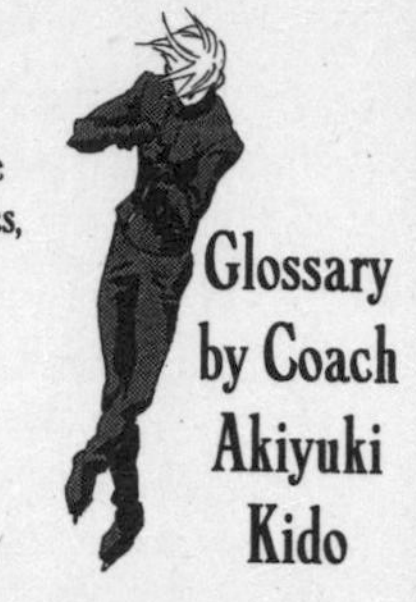

Glossary by Coach Akiyuki Kido

National Figure Skating Championships (page 15)
The Japan Figure Skating Championships are held every year near the end of December to determine the best skater in Japan. This competition doubles as the qualifying event to represent Japan at the Olympics, World Championships, and Four Continents Championships.

ISU Grand Prix Final (page 16)
The ISU Grand Prix is a series of six competitions held between October and December, including Skate America, Skate Canada, the Cup of China, the Trophée Eric Bompard (France), the Rostelecom Cup (Russia), and the NHK Trophy (Japan). The order they're held in varies by year. The six highest-ranking skaters go on to compete in the Grand Prix Final.

One-foot Axel (page 17)
Normally when performing an Axel, a skater jumps from their left skate's forward outside edge and lands on their right skate's back outside edge. For a one-foot Axel, a skater jumps from their right skate's forward inside edge and lands on their right skate's back outside edge.

Rocker (page 17)
This turn is similar to a three turn (a turn that traces a path resembling the number three), but its curve changes direction. As a result, it can be executed on a single edge.

Inside edge (page 17)
The bottom of an ice skate's blade has a semicircular hollow with two edges. The inside edge is the one between the skater's legs.

Level four (page 17)
Elements such as lifts, steps, twizzles, and dance spins are categorized into levels on the basis of certain features. An element with a higher level has a higher base value in scoring, and the highest level is four. World-class skaters perform most elements at level four.

Trainer (page 28)
A trainer works to improve a skater's condition and make them more competitive by providing support and guidance to improve their physical fitness, psychological resilience, and overall health.

Open practice (page 37)
Open practice is typically held on the day before or the day of a competition. It's the skaters' last chance to polish their routines, and they're free to participate or not at their discretion. The technical panel—which consists of a technical specialist, an assistant technical specialist, and a technical controller—is required to watch and familiarize themselves with the skaters' programs.

Short program (page 40)
The short program is a segment in which the skaters have up to two minutes and fifty seconds to perform eight predetermined elements, such as jumps, spins, or steps.

Group four (page 40)
This refers to the fourth group of skaters. In the free skate, the first group to skate is made up of the skaters who scored the lowest in the short program, and the last group is made up of the skaters who scored the highest.

Start order/Number X (page 40)
The order in which skaters perform is determined by random draw at the beginning of the competition. For the free skate, skaters are divided into groups of no more than six based on their placement in the short program. Within each group, the start order is determined by random draw.

World Championships (page 41)
The World Figure Skating Championships is the biggest event of the skating season, excluding the Olympics. The winner earns the title of world champion for that season.

Junior Championships (page 41)
The Japan Junior Figure Skating Championships are a competition held toward the end of November to determine the best junior figure skater in Japan. The winner can earn the opportunity to compete in the next senior championships.

Triple Axel (page 42)
There are six different jumps in figure skating. An Axel is the only one that begins with the skater facing directly forward. It's the most difficult jump, and a triple Axel requires three and a half midair rotations. Midori Ito was the first woman in Japan to successfully execute this jump.

Clean landing (page 42)
If a skater lands a jump smoothly and correctly, their landing is clean.

Bonus points (page 42)
Each element—such as a jump, spin, step sequence, or spiral sequence—has a base value for use in scoring. The judges assign a modifier with one of seven values between negative and positive three to this base value, resulting in either a deduction or bonus points. Today, these deductions and bonuses are clearly defined in the rules, and there is a checklist of features that will earn one or the other (e.g., particularly high or low jumps, the overall flow, speed, etc.).

Flip (page 43)
To perform this jump, the skater uses their right toe to launch themselves into the air from their left skate's back inside edge. It is sometimes called the toe Salchow. (Note that the roles of each foot are reversed if the skater is going to rotate in the opposite direction.)

Loop (page 43)
For this jump, the skater both takes off from and lands on only their right foot. With their left leg crossed in front of their right, they jump from the right skate's back outside edge.

Step (page 43)
A step is a kind of footwork that a skater can weave in with elements such as turns. Moves such as the Mohawk, the chasse, the crossroll, and the Choctaw are steps, whereas the three turn, loop turn, rocker, counter, bracket, and twizzle are turns. A combination of steps and turns is called a step sequence.

Salchow (page 43)
This jump is executed from the left foot's back inside edge by lifting the right foot forward and to the left. The way both feet face outward just before takeoff is a unique feature of the Salchow jump. It was named after the Swedish skater Ulrich Salchow.

Spin (page 43)
A spin involves rotating in place on one leg. Spins are scored on the basis of factors such as the number of rotations, the aesthetic quality of the posture, and the difficulty of the pose.

Toe loop (page 49)
The toe loop is considered to be the the easiest jump. The skater uses their left toe to launch themselves into the air from their right skate's back outside edge. To date, no one has managed to execute this jump with more than four revolutions, and only a select few skaters can do even that.

Coach (page 53)
A coach can be someone who belongs to the Figure Skating Instructor Association, or someone who just works at a particular ice rink. To work as a professional coach, even talented skaters are typically required to start by helping to teach beginners in a club or classroom setting.

NHK Trophy (page 54)
This is one of the competitions in the ISU Grand Prix.

Free skate (page 54)
In the free skating competition, skaters get to choose what elements and moves to use. Still, to ensure a well-rounded program, there are rules about what jumps, spins, and steps are required, as well as restrictions on the number of them allowed. In women's singles, this segment lasts four minutes, and in men's singles, it lasts four minutes and thirty seconds.

Combination (page 55)
A jump combination is when a skater performs a jump and then immediately performs another one from the foot they land on. Since jumps are landed on the right skate's back outside edge (or the left skate's, if spinning clockwise), all jumps after the first in a combination are limited to either the toe loop or the loop jump. If a skater weaves steps between their jumps, it's called a jump sequence instead.

Required jumps (page 57)
The six jumps in figure skating are the toe loop, Salchow, loop, flip, Lutz, and Axel. In the short program, the following jumps are required:
1) a triple-triple or triple-double jump combination,
2) a triple jump following a step, and
3) a double or triple Axel.
In the free skate, the skater may perform up to eight jumps, one of which must be an Axel.
No more than three jump combinations are allowed, and only one of those can consist of three jumps.

Technical score (page 57)
The technical score is determined by the technical elements included in the program and their quality. Jumps, spins, steps, and other elements each have a base value, which is modified by a grade of execution (GOE) to get the technical score. The GOE is the average of the modifiers assigned by the judges, excluding the highest and lowest. These modifiers have one of seven values between negative and positive three.

Program components score (presentation score) (page 57)
For this score, skaters are evaluated on the basis of five program components: skating skills, transitions, performance, composition, and interpre-tation. In ice dancing's compulsory dance, there are instead four components: skating skills, performance, interpretation, and timing. A skater's final score is the total of their program components score (PCS) and their technical score.

4T (page 67)
This is the abbreviation for a quadruple toe loop. The abbreviation for a Salchow is S, for a loop is Lo, for a flip is F, for a Lutz is Lz, and for an Axel is A.

Lutz (page 73)
The Lutz is the second hardest jump after the Axel. To perform this jump, a skater uses their right toe pick (the front of the skate's blade, where it has teeth) to launch themselves into the air from their left skate's back outside edge. It is named after the Austrian skater Alois Lutz, the first person to perform this jump. (Note that the roles of each foot are reversed if the skater is going to rotate in the opposite direction.)

Base value (page 75)
Each element—such as a step, a spin, or a jump—has a base value. Three people—the technical specialist, the assistant technical specialist, and the technical controller—work together to do things like identify elements, count jump rotations, and distinguish the level and type of each spin or step. These determinations result in the assignment of a base score.

Hand touching the ice (page 88)
A skater touching the ice with a hand on a landing is the next most serious error after a fall.

Four Continents Championships (4CC) (page 142)
The Four Continents Figure Skating Championships is an international competition open to skaters from four continents: Africa, Asia, the Americas, and Oceania. Europe is excluded.

Ice dancing (page 151)
Alongside singles and pairs, ice dancing is another category of competitive figure skating. Skaters participate in teams consisting of one man and one woman. Its origins lie in ballroom dancing, and it has a beautiful and unique style. Rhythm, musicality, and footwork are given priority in ice dancing, and there are those who argue that it requires the most skill of any kind of figure skating competition.

Season's best (page 166)
This term refers to a given skater's highest score of the season.

Akiyuki Kido
Born on August 28th, 1975, Akiyuki Kido represented Japan in ice dancing at the 2006 Winter Olympics in Turin, Italy. He took fifteenth place, the highest Japan had ever placed in ice dancing at the time. Today, he works as a coach at the Shin-Yokohama Skate Center.

Knight of the Ice Skater Profile 2

2	Raito Tamura

Height:

172 cm

Blood type:

O

Birthday:

October 12th

Place of origin:

Aichi Prefecture

Strongest element:

Spins

Strongest jump:

Salchow

Most difficult jump performed to date:

Triple Axel

Strength:

His passionate self-expression and flexibility

Weakness:

He's tone deaf, so the more feeling he puts into his skating, the more he deviates from the music

Hobby:

Bath-time skincare

Talent:

Identifying people and objects by smell

Family composition:

Two parents and a younger brother

Favorite food:

Lychee berries (publically), Garigari-kun popsicles (secretly)

Least favorite food:

Junk food (publically), tomatoes (secretly)

Notes:

His coach is his grandfather, Masato Tamura. Although Raito is aware of his own tone deafness, he still loves karaoke. He's not very good at English, and he's prone to sneezing and getting a runny nose.

Divided Opinion

Episode 1
Virgin: Yes or No?

I was surprised to find how many people agreed he was a virgin when I asked their opinions... Maybe the virgins ... if they can find the courage to be open about it... Who knows?

THE DAY DREW EVER CLOSER, AND SOON ENOUGH...
...IT WAS TIME TO SEE WHO WOULD BE THIS SEASON'S WORLD CHAMPION.
NICE COTE AZUR

next volume...

I WANT TO OBSERVE THAT SKATER FIRST.

Knight of the Ice 3

Coming soon!

How will Chitose answer Kokoro's sudden and shocking proposition?! Plus, it's finally time for the World Championships in Nice, France, where Kokoro and the rest of the Japanese team will have to go up against some powerhouses from abroad! And what will happen when Chitose the trainer has an accident...?

A SMART, NEW ROMANTIC COMEDY FOR FANS OF *SHORTCAKE CAKE* AND *TERRACE HOUSE*!

LIVING-ROOM MATSUNAGA-SAN

1

Keiko Iwashita

A romance manga starring high school girl Meeko, who learns to live on her own in a boarding house whose living room is home to the odd (but handsome) Matsunaga-san. She begins to adjust to her new life away from her parents, but Meeko soon learns that no matter how far away from home she is, she's still a young girl at heart — especially when she finds herself falling for Matsunaga-san.

Knight of the Ice 2 is a work of fiction. Names, characters, places, and incidents are the products of the author's imagination or are used fictitiously. Any resemblance to actual events, locales, or persons, living or dead, is entirely coincidental.

A Kodansha Comics Trade Paperback Original

Published in the United States by Kodansha Comics, an imprint of Kodansha USA Publishing, LLC, New York.

Publication rights for this English edition arranged through Kodansha Ltd., Tokyo.

First published in Japan in 2013 by Kodansha Ltd., Tokyo as *Ginban Kishi*, volume 2.

ISBN 978-1-63236-962-8

Printed in the United States of America.

www.kodanshacomics.com

9 8 7 6 5 4 3 2 1
Translation: Rose Padgett
Lettering: Jennifer Skarupa
Editing: Tiff Ferentini
Kodansha Comics edition cover design by Phil Balsman

Publisher: Kiichiro Sugawara
Vice president of marketing & publicity: Naho Yamada

Director of publishing services: Ben Applegate
Associate director of operations: Stephen Pakula
Publishing services managing editor: Noelle Webster
Assistant production manager: Emi Lotto, Angela Zurlo